The Power of Knowing:

8 Step Guide to Open Your Intuitive Channel and Live in Highest Consciousness - Clarity, peace, power and transformation

A Non-fiction Book

by

Jean Walters, DM, DD, CRT
A professional psychic for 40 years

Higher Ground Books & Media
Springfield, Ohio.
http://www.highergroundbooksandmedia.com

Printed in the United States of America 2020

The Power of Knowing:

8 Step Guide to Open Your Intuitive Channel and Live in Highest Consciousness - Clarity, peace, power and transformation

A Non-fiction Book

by

Jean Walters, DM, DD, CRT
A professional psychic for 40 years

jean@spiritualtransformation.com
http://www.spiritualtransformation.com

Reviews for The Power of KNOWING

If you are on a spiritual journey to find your True (Higher) Self, *The Power of KNOWING* will give you the motivation to persist. Jean Walters offers inspiration and activities to reconnect with Spirit and Light, a connection many have lost because of the mental clutter of the ego and the pressure to focus on external validation instead of inner meaning. Self-mastery is achievable, but difficult. Not everyone can accomplish it. This book is like having Jean at your side, as a supportive friend and mentor.

Lucy Knapp, Editor, St. Louis & St. Charles Women's Journal

Another home run for Jean Walters... Her *Power of KNOWING* just might be a grand slam. I love the chapter on Making the Connection: Fear of Failure because it helped me diminish egoic thought patterns. Also, understanding that Everything is Energy clarified some important issues, like how we are drawn to certain people and events. Thank you, Jean for writing another great book and the right techniques to achieve self-mastery.

Karen Hoffman, Founder Gateway to Dreams; www.gatewaytodreams.org

The Power of KNOWING is aptly titled because through this book you learn how powerful you really are. Jean shares her vast knowledge with you through activities at the end of each chapter, which enables you to build your metaphysical skills. It is a great resource for those who want to develop and grow in spiritual depth.

Mary Bryant Miller, Educator, Librarian, and Student of Metaphysics

I loved this book. Jean's writings speak directly to my mind and heart. She has a simple and easy way of explaining profound and life changing topics. *The Power of KNOWING* is an important reminder that I am more than my pedigree career, age, or body type. I think you can call this book *the Key to Living in Vastness*. Thank you, Jean

Melody Murray, Owner of Take the Back Skin Care and Real World Coaching

The Power of KNOWING is one of those books you will want to keep and refer to many times. Jean Walters shares her wisdom of self-mastery with generosity and honesty. Each chapter presents practical applications that are life transforming, leading to more joy, love, and peace. It is a handbook for transformation in our troubled world

Donna Hasegawa MFA ATR-BC, abstractartisthasegawa.com

About 20 years ago, I was going through a transitional part of my life and I had a prayer that I prayed daily; "I know I am supposed to learn something, I know that this is a growth opportunity. Send me teachers; send me help. I am willing to do the work." Jean Walters showed up one day and sent me down a path that perfectly suited my needs. It is my sincere wish that she do the same for you with this book and all her work. But you need to be willing to do the work!

Rich Dalton (radio rich), St. Louis radio host, producer, and musician

Anything is possible when you set your intention and follow your intuition. *The Power of KNOWING* provides amazing techniques to get in touch with your intuitive mind. Jean teaches in a way that is easy to understand so you can apply these principles to your life. With practice following these action steps, YOU have the ability to transform your life.

Mary Taykowski, High Risk Nurse Case Manager

Jean Walters offers us insight and self-possession in her book, *The Power of KNOWING: Eight Ways to Connect to Your Higher Self for Clarity and Confidence.*
She also provides real steps to be taken in our own spiritual quest. And, her book entertains with stories, anecdotes and vignettes drawn from her life and the life of others, great and small. Jean leaves me yearning to harness my own Power of KNOWING every day in every way.

Jan Kraus, Technology professional, consultant, writer, searcher and artist.

In *The Power of KNOWING*, Jean Walters infuses her words with love – love of highest self and others. As she unfolds her understanding of the human condition, she leads the reader to consider self in relation to the big picture. Knowing self becomes the focus, and that focus leads readers to lives of awareness, peace, love and acceptance of self. The suggested exercises bring each one who practices them to places of thoughtful reflection – reflections which yield fuller, more significant life experiences.
Jean makes it clear that we can know self, a goal that has been relegated to an inconvenience by many in this world of pragmatic materialism. Through the ages sages have insisted that knowledge of self is no secondary consideration. The Oracle at Delphi boldly displayed these words: *Know Thyself.* Alexander Pope, in the early 18th century, declared, *"Know then, thyself..."* Jean Walters helps the reader to that revered end.

Michael DePung, author of *Discover Self, Create Purpose: Superhero You*

Jean Walters' new book *The Power of Knowing* provides the first of its kind step-by-step guide to help you tap into and sustain your intuition. We've all flashes of insight or a sense of knowing, but our ability to easily connect and use our intuition to make better choices is often elusive. Jean combines insightful stories with practical actions that help develop our intuitive muscle so that we can step into our lives with greater confidence and sense of purpose.

Debbie Josendale, Owner of Captivate & Company, Marketing and Strategies

Most of us don't trust ourselves and this leads to anxiety, stress, and a worrisome life. Jean's book guides us back to that "still small voice" that Knows the next right step. Jean offers methods and techniques to expand our consciousness, actually allowing us to surrender to the unknown and free ourselves from the ego's push for more. By following her 8 outlined ways, we can let go of the need to protect ourselves and be "safe" and reclaim the innocence and fascination we had as a child.

Angie Monko, Owner of Harmony Harbor Coaching

I have known, been counseled and studied under Jean Walters direction for more years than I can count! What a divine "Master" God has bestowed us with! There is not a measure of words to express the direction and guidance her brilliant intellect has had upon my life and journey. Jean's beautiful wisdom and mastery, provide an immersion into life, heart and soul…and if you so dare bring forth the courage to delve into those places yet undiscovered within, you will find her words have a profound way of guiding you through the journey. As you embark down your path, it is easy to see how much our beliefs directly influence our earthly experience. Jean's depth of understanding and wisdom shared in her beautiful books, talk shows or lectures, will show you an enlightened way of thinking, engaging and courage that reflects the simple truths and spiritual lessons needed to full fill and impact whatever questions, uncharted waters and thoughts you may have as you pave the road ahead.

~ Madeleine Prewitt, Owner, Bee Beautiful Life Styles, a boutique life style company specializing in design and event planning

Table of Contents

Someone Who Found His Purpose in Love

Foreword

Happiness, peace, and inner knowing do not have to be happenstance or mysterious, and they certainly are not out of reach. You have an inner intuitive voice that can be cultivated and a dynamic mind that holds no limits. When these are properly trained and directed, you have the ability to live and express a miraculous and powerful reality.

Our mental capacity is vast. We have not even scratched the surface of what is possible. There are enlightened masters walking the earth who everyday perform miracles, the least of these to manifest gold and jewels from thin air (Sai Baba in India). The most profound to reconstruct spiritual DNA evoking deep inner healing from trauma, helping crippled people walk, heart conditions to heal, tumors to disappear, and barren women to birth children.

In these last instances I refer to the work of Medium Joao of Brazil, otherwise known as John of God, who weekly relinquished his body to exalted masters and healers who ministered to millions of people from all over the world. In these material and spiritual transformations, a man bound to a wheelchair for 50 years was able to stand up and walk; a woman in need of a liver transplant is supplied, along with the name of the donor. All within an evening's work. And others are cleansed of anger, negative judgments, psychological wounds, and addictions.

This book will not instruct you on how to incorporate master healers into your body. But it will assist you in intensifying a channel of Light energy within that will guide you to a life of depth, clarity, purpose and connection. It will provide instruction on how to connect to Highest Energy – High Self, Super Conscious Mind, Christ Consciousness, love, call it what you will. It is about accessing the power of your soul, becoming the dynamic being you've been designed to be, and taking your place in this time of spiritual evolution to play the part you are meant to play and, in so doing, blessing the world.

Spiritual evolution is a step-by-step process. You can't wish for it or pray for it and not be active in the process of attaining it. In this manuscript I provide steps and processes that I have used and developed personally with thousands of students for 40+ years.

I have a unique ability to break down seemingly complicated processes rendering them comprehensible and applicable. I understand the workings of spirit and universal law and it is my purpose to educate and share this life-changing information.

Throughout my career I have presented approximately 35,000 Akashic Record Readings to people all over the world. My purpose has been to provide deep insight to facilitate healing; clarity to assist in making decisions, planning, and strategizing; help in repairing or releasing relationships; and understanding as to cause-effect conditions in optimizing health.

Along the way I have detected health issues that could be repaired (healed), impending death and/or birth, past life situations that reveal information for healing present circumstances and relationships; and lots of assistance in helping people change, evolve and grow. In fact, that has always been my focus – growth - and that is what this manuscript is about. The Bible says, the truth shall set you free and it will!

We are magnificent, spiritual being and have the ability to move mountains (challenges), but to do that we must train the mind to do our bidding. The mind is a tool that we can hone. Just as we don't want other people, our work or outer conditions to run us, we shouldn't allow our egoic, chaotic, intellectual minds to do that either. That is what I offer you in these pages. The opportunity to take control and make peace and clarity your highest priority. That is how you bring the best to those you love and that is how you learn to live in love and peace - our highest state of being.

In this manuscript, I am your guide to set up an internal environment to nurture inner knowing and deepest connection. As we do this work, you will begin to realize your inherent power as a spiritual being and, in all probability, have fun along the way.

The key to moving beyond the reasoning, analytical, limited mind of the human ego is to connect with the intuitive, feeling mind of the soul. Yes, everyone can do this. Everyone has the capacity. It takes practice and letting go and cleaning out old, staid beliefs that do not serve.

Everyone has a purpose and inner map to soul fulfillment. By utilizing the methods described herein, you will be led along your path of divine inspiration and expression. You can know your purpose and why you are here. You can fulfill your spiritual directive with joy, abundance, and peace. There are myriad stories illustrating these points (we learn best through stories) and what is possible when the mind is focused with clear intention. That is how we will begin, by establishing clear intent.

About Jean Walters

Jean Walters has been a truth seeker since she was nine years old and first saw a brilliant white light that channeled through her body from the top of her head to the toes of her feet. She observed this Light as beautiful, joyful and constant and understood it to be her true self. Her curiosity to understand this Light energy that never changed and was always available, led her to study spirituality, metaphysics, meditation, universal law, the Vedantas, the Bhagavad Gita, A Course in Miracles, the Bible, and many other sacred texts.

This study has led to a forty-year career of adventure and exploration and willingness to take the next step and climb the next mountain of discovery. She has developed and used her intuitive channel in service and as a way of understanding that the inherent purpose of each person is to express.

Over the years she has shared truth as a transformational coach, given over 35,000 Akashic Record (psychic) readings for people all over the world, written columns and articles for major newspapers, and magazines, and had a syndicated radio show called, *Positive Moments*. Through her work she has helped heal relationships and situations by providing insight, vision, and inspiring highest action. In her process she has developed the ability to access highest energy and information at will and has instructed many others to do the same. To touch people all over the world through her work has been a dream come true. It is the fulfillment of her mission.

Introduction – Opening the Door to Knowing

What lies behind us and what lies before us are tiny matters, compared to what lies within us.

Oliver Wendell Holmes

Think about the times in your life when you've had flashes of "knowing" -- those wonderful moments of clarity when you were incredibly confident about what to do or how to solve a problem.

You just KNEW.

You knew it was time to go back to school, purchase your home, get into a relationship, get out of a relationship, invest money, become a vegetarian, buy a lottery ticket, or call your friend. And, because you acted in that moment of clarity, things turned out well and your life transformed. It was as if some invisible force or friend was guiding you.

Here is an example:

Jack was called into the office at work and informed that his job had been terminated. At first, he argued, but then he stopped because a voice inside him said, *"It is time to go. There are greener pastures ahead."* And, with that knowing, Jack raised himself up, accepted his last paycheck, shook the hand of his former employer, and left. At the time, he didn't know what these greener pastures were, but Jack trusted the voice.

The following week, Jack's friend, John, called to tell him that he was starting a home repair business and wanted Jack to be his partner. Jack had always wanted to be self-employed and John was the perfect partner. He was ambitious and visionary, and they complemented each other's diverse skill sets. So, just like that, Jack said, *"YES,"* and never looked back. He had found his greener pasture.

The same thing happens all the time – with health, wealth, relationships, where to go on vacation, what job to take, what food to eat, which way to turn, and so forth. We have a *voice* inside that KNOWS. It is our connection to something greater than this moment. It is a resource that never goes away and can always be trusted. You can nurture this connection and it can become your everyday resource to a life of brilliance and joy.

Material sense can never and will never reveal the perpetual harmony we desire. Intuition is the spiritual faculty and quality that takes us to our Promised Land of abundance, peace, and truth. As we develop this skill, we put aside the old self that judges by appearances and memorizes facts so that we can build the new self who intuitively perceives the reality behind the mask of personality and form. The result we seek is vision, clarity, and greater purpose.

That is what this book is about – becoming receptive to that voice and learning to trust it.

Implicitly.

When I was beginning to learn about spirituality and metaphysics, I signed on for a program to understand the mind and how it works. Part of the curriculum was to develop concentration and focus. Most people have incredible difficulty focusing. They tend to be scattered, letting the mind wander wantonly all over the place, changing from one subject to another without any orientation. Their ability to hold attention and manage the type of thoughts they want to generate is severely lacking. They are also inclined to believe that what they think has no relevance to what happens in their lives. Nothing could be further from the truth. There is a direct correlation between what you think and the quality of your life.

This leads to the power of connection, which naturally moves you to the power of knowing. Why is managing the mind so difficult and why is it so important? Because having strong concentration makes it possible to connect to your Highest Self and access strong, indisputable intuition, which shines a light on where you are to go and what you are to do. It is your guide to living an exalted life.

Intuition is the voice of God speaking through you. It is the way you are constantly connected to your Source. To live from a high state of intuitive energy sets you at a huge advantage in life. You cut out a lot of superfluous effort and wasted time to reach your goals. You develop a "big picture" approach and understand the "real" purpose behind events in your
life.

Achieving this pinnacle of mastery involves conditioning and training. You become receptive, learn to listen, and develop the discipline to maintain focus and set clear intentions. You release scattered thinking and negativity. In the process, you acquire the ability to *see* beyond present circumstances and recognize the bigger picture.

Let's not get confused. Growth happens when we experience the chaos of earth and address it with a centered mind that accesses possibilities as opportunities. Even though fear is present, the advanced soul moves forward. For what is it to be lost – a lifestyle, money, relationship, job, home. All of these can and will be replaced. But that cannot happen until you let go. The pseudo identities of status, fame, possessions and tribe are temporal and disposable. It is in the courage to change that transformation takes place. We cannot ascend to higher consciousness without the willingness to release that which was and has been.

Struggle is the ego's way of resisting change. It can keep us stuck in the muddled mind. Yet when we begin to look beyond the moment and the fear of loss, we can perceive a greater possibility just ahead.

The outer adjusts to our new frame of reference. Expansion occurs when we greet new opportunity with an open-heart setting fear aside. Our inner knowing engages in sure footedness.

There is no loss for we are greater than we were before. That is what growth is about.

The age-old questions are: Why am I here? What is my purpose? How can I achieve fulfillment? Many want a map or at least a set of directions to figure these things out. In this book, I provide the next closest thing, a set of principles, methods, and techniques that work to connect you with your spiritual center and uncover your answers.

Cultivating these skills brings you peace and confidence. As you begin this journey, you will discover things about yourself, learn to be objective, give up demeaning ego blame and shame, and develop the ability to live from an internal place of power.

Here is an example:

In the 1960s a Harvard psychology professor named Richard Albert set out on a journey of self-discovery. He was looking for *his* answers. From a worldly perspective, he had achieved a lot, but it wasn't enough. He was not happy.

Albert had already realized that he could not find his answers in a book, another academic degree, having more money, or buying a newer, fancier car. He knew he needed to change his focus and search in different ways. As a result, Albert ended up in India, standing before a holy man, who, in a few words, shredded his former life and identity as a rich man, educator, collector of things, and researcher to become a teacher of love, author of the book *Be Here Now,* and founder of the Seva charitable foundation. This guru (teacher) looked into Albert's soul, witnessed his shame and guilt, and loved him anyway. It was the most profound experience of Richard Albert's life, and when he departed India, he had become a new person with a new purpose, and a new name, Ram Dass, which means *"servant of God."*

In Albert's case, he was prepared to shed old ways. He wanted transformation. He had studied consciousness for much of his life and was ready to pursue a higher path. Sometimes you have to exhaust all other methods before the time has come to follow a spiritual path. Sometimes you have to be at the bottom before you can rise up.

Readiness is an individual matter. You are the one to decide when and if you are to transform by accessing your higher mind. When you are truly ready, as with Albert, you will find the answers you seek.

In this book, I offer methods to actively expand your consciousness. As you utilize these, you will learn how to refine your focus and access wisdom, insight, and mastery. Remember the axiom – the truth will set you free? Well, it's true!

As you progress, you will heal your neurological system. It has been damaged by anxiety, fear, and wrong focus. As your nervous system gets stronger, you will be able to open to deeper, finer levels of energy making intuitive wisdom available to you. You will become a channel for Light.

This manuscript is divided into eight sections. Each one introduces a different aspect of this evolutionary process along with practical tools and exercises to increase mental strength and awareness.

Add them all up and they lead to trust.

Self-trust.

This means you have strengthened your intuitive connection and accessed your still small voice, the voice of knowing, and you are ready to be guided. This is the same thing that Physicist, Albert Einstein, spoke of when he stated, *"The years of anxious searching in the dark, with their intense longing, their alternations of confidence and exhaustion, and final emergence into light – only those who have experienced it can understand that."*

The final section will help you incorporate what you've discovered into daily practice. The suggested daily action plan will help you strengthen your intuitive muscle and increase self-awareness. You are actively shifting your focus to higher consciousness. Taking daily action steps will support your ability to discover and implement your new power in all areas of life.

You have the ability to develop a strong connection to Source energy and deepest knowing. The information and exercises described herein outlines a step-by-step approach that will raise your consciousness and tap into Infinite Intelligence. As you take these steps, you will have forever tools that move you beyond intellectual knowledge and bring you face to face with answers, solutions, and connection to Highest Consciousness and a better you.

My mission is to help you return to the loving center you have always had.

Accomplishing this requires softening your approach to life and developing in-depth listening skills. In time, your inner voice will increase in volume and becomes a steadfast, trustworthy guide. Your ability to discern the nature of events and their true meaning will increase along with self-trust and your confidence will soar.

I. The Beginning

Darkness cannot drive out darkness; only light can do that.
Hate cannot drive out hate; only love can do that.

Martin Luther King Jr.

Summary: We came into life knowing how to be happy and vibrant and now it is time to move from our slow grasping caterpillar mentality to the transformational quality of our inner butterfly. This means we concentrate attention on depth and heart-felt desires that connect with the quantum field of energy in which we live and breathe. This takes us from our small egoic boundaries into the vast inspired consciousness that guides us from limitation into greatness.

Stories of great leaders who used the power of focus and commitment to fulfill their purposes are offered as illustration of the inherent power we all possess.

How we lost focus and how to get it back gives the history and biology of how we got off track and what we need to do to reestablish focus and control.

Understanding cause and effect and how it shows up in every situation begins the instruction to achieve higher vision. This section concludes with the principle of natural expansion and how it works in your life and how to recognize your intuitive voice

***

If you have ever felt empty or emotionally out of control, you have been given the signal – it is time to make some changes. We have lost much in our journey through life – innocence, faith, vision, confidence, and openness. As we begin our process of transformation, we will make the necessary course corrections and we reclaim these qualities.

In this study, you seek to comprehend the soul path you have chosen. This starts with understanding yourself, how you created your identity, and what it takes to connect with your deepest essence. You must take command of your mind. This alone yields dynamic results that lead you on your path of mastering intuition. In this section, you begin with the first step.

***

Your Call to Connect – First Step

Is it time to make changes… to shift your focus? Perhaps you need a larger picture, and the confidence to do what needs to be done no matter what. The process is transformative. Much like the caterpillar spinning a chrysalis to prepare for new life in the form of a butterfly, you are about to return to the memory of innocence, when life was fascinating, and everything was possible. It is your pure state of spiritual connection and knowing. It is the beginning.

Babies find life fascinating. Every color and shape draws delighted smiles and coos – sometimes even screams of delight. As they grow, babies scramble to discover what hides in the wastebasket or on top of the shelf. They climb with abandon, seeking the next fascination. Hands in soap, mud or spit up – it is all the same -- a texture to explore or taste. They listen, touch, taste and smell. It is their process. They are unconfined by convention. Nor are they littered with mental constructs of limitation and fear. The inner need to discover, experiment, and experience is the freedom of the soul and this drive is alive within you as well. Returning to Spiritual freedom is our quest!

As we develop, we learn through play. Children know how to play. They jump out of bed and know just what to do. Whether it is to challenge their friend to a game of skipping pebbles across the pond, or build a fort, or climb a tree, they are driven to adventure and their minds are open for what comes next. Children are beautiful, uncluttered, innocent and without knowledge. Yet, they are excited and willing to learn. They are shameless and guiltless in their urge for discovery.

Before a child is programmed with the need for specific results, they approach life as a grand vista of opportunity – an adventure. What happens to dissuade this desire to venture into the unknown? What happens to daunt the spirit of curiosity? How did we forget to ask: What lies over the next hill? How do I get there?

When do we lose the desire to enter the unidentified, and become enamored instead with the concept of safety? How did we buy into the idea of building some sort of kingdom to hide in and imagine life as a dangerous foe to battle and resist?

So, we ask, what is the way to relearn what it is to live expansively in the way of a child and open to the magic of curiosity, optimism and possibility? This is what we seek as we explore practices and techniques to achieve mastery, knowing, and connection.

Directing your powerful mind is the key and the most important element in constructing this skill of on-going, never-failing connection. Your mind has the power to move mountains. When Jesus instructed his followers to have faith the size of a mustard seed and you can move mountains (challenges), he meant to have focused mental control so that when you fix on a goal, you are assured of achieving it. When you set this resolve, the field of energy in which you live (the Quantum Field) has no alternative but to do your bidding. That also means that when you set your focus on limitation, the Quantum Field unerringly follows your directive. Thus, whatever you focus on (positive or negative), you will achieve. Henry Ford said it best, *if you think you can or you think you can't, you are right.* What is it you truly want? On what are you *willing* to maintain focus?

This capacity of concentrated focus is obvious with great leaders. We saw it in the leadership of Nelson Mandela, who never forgot his vision of *one person, one vote* when he stood against Apartheid in South Africa. He never forgot even when he was jailed for 25 years. Upon his eventual release, Mandela continued his quest for equality for all South Africans. He maintained his focus and won.

The great Indian leader, Mohandas Gandhi, was clear on his mission of procuring freedom from British rule for India. He held his ideal and spoke to the masses despite crippling shyness, fear of speaking before groups, and massive British resistance. He overrode fear with clear vision and a mission bigger than himself and walked forward despite his awkwardness.

Boxing great, Mohammed Ali's proclamation, *I'm the greatest*, was revolutionary for that time. It carried him to win an Olympic gold medal, become a Golden Glove Champion, and the Heavy Weight Champion of the world. The strength of his determination is legendary.

Each of these leaders exemplifies the principle of unwavering focus. Each had many ups and downs along his path to achievement. Yet each accomplished his goal despite obstacles. You can do the same.

When we observe a person that will not be dissuaded from his objective, we witness greatness. This formula for attainment is in the control of every person. When we set the mind to achieve, while refusing distraction, mountains (obstacles) are moved.

Unfortunately, we often witness this phenomenal power misdirected with affirmations such as, *I'm really old, I never feel good, I'll never be able to do that,* or *I always struggle with money.* And with these statements, we find the people uttering them fulfilling their self-determined directives because each has placed his faith in that particular outcome.

So again, the question, what do you want and what are you willing to do to get it? Are you willing to release self-limiting thoughts to move your mountain?

Activity

Pick an objective on which to focus. Example – a new car, organize the garage, clarity about the next step for your business. As you maintain focus, you will begin to notice opportunities to take action on this goal. For instance, you may see an advertisement on the type of car you want greatly discounted, or a friend decides to sell his car and it just happens to be exactly what you are looking for. Perhaps you discover a store that sells everything necessary to organize your garage. Or you run into a friend who has a similar business to yours and tells you of a new marketing plan or consultant that has been helpful.

In each instant, when you keep your antenna up (pay attention), you develop heightened awareness and instead of thinking that these opportunities are coincidences, you realize that you attracted these people and events because you were clear in your intention. This is exactly the same way it worked for Mandela, Gandhi, and Ali.

***

How We Lost Focus and How to get it Back

From time immemorial man has searched for the meaning of life. We have searched because we have formed a false sense of identity. In the beginning, as infants, we radiated love. As we looked at the world and the people around us, we were enthralled. At that time, we were still aware of our Inner Source of Love, so we could gaze at the material world without judgment or attachment. We saw it with the eyes of wonder and fascination. Everything was amazing – people, sounds, shapes, and forms. There was no judgment. We drank it up with relish and awe.

It was fun!

Then something happened.

Over time, we were informed that we were to be identified as Johnny, Suzi, Mary, or whoever. We were also told that we were good boys or girls or bad boys or girls depending on someone else's opinion and needs. We began to fall into these descriptions and shaped our self-concept accordingly. We formulated our personality and behaviors to fit this mold as well.

Soon there was an identity -- a body, a toy, an opinion, a set of circumstances…. my room, my bed, my toy, my mom, my ethnic group, etc. We were even educated and cultivated on what to believe – what were the correct precepts, who we were to like or disdain, and how to define God. We even put God out there, far away, in the sky, unattainable.

Day-by-day we took this program in and developed a sense of self. As we did this, we formulated limitation and restriction and we no longer believed we could climb the highest hill and move mountains. We got distracted. It was our error and it was grave.

We bought into the idea that we would survive if we were confirmed "good." It translated to mean we were acceptable. Thus, our views regarding shape, color, size, intelligence, and worthiness took form from these concepts. This is how our focus turned outward to the external world and we believed that our source for love were the people around us – our parents, siblings, peers, friends, employers, and so forth. The idea of proving our worthiness was born. Our safety, indeed, survival, teetered on these things. That is what we believed, and we were wrong.

If something altered our reality such as death, divorce, changing jobs or locations, our security was challenged. It could even crumble. Where is my toy, my friend, my room? Soon, we are hooked by the material world and completely sidetracked from our inner Light, our eternal source of love and joy. That which at one point made us complete, seemed to have disappeared, its value no longer registered in our consciousness. It was not the popular or encouraged focus and we shifted to being accepted by those around us. We turned our attention from our inner world of curiosity and adventure to the external world of achievement, accumulation, and winning, and we began to feel anxious and insecure. Why? Because these goals will never be enough. The material world is unstable and never secure. It is always shifting and changing - never constant.

That is when we started looking to tangible accomplishment to discover a loftier reality.

If I had the right education, made more money, owned a bigger house, a faster car, then I would feel stronger, more loved and safe. This incessant race after things produced restlessness and lack of fulfillment because no matter what, it was never enough. Security was never locked down.

The happiness that followed each event or accomplishment was short-lived, only to be replaced with another quest. By this time, we are stuck in the sensory, material world. Our recognition of self-worth dependent on the grades we receive, the brand of clothes we wear, the roles we play, level of popularity, and if we are pretty or thin enough, and associated with the right tribe. We lost our self. We were sidetracked – distracted from our center, our connection with the Universe, our inner Light. A consciousness that is conditioned to identify with form (the physical body, job or career, quality of education, and possessions) will find awareness of inner space impossible. Yet this can be remedied.

It means to experience the *"peace that goes beyond understanding,"* you must shift your focus and reestablish your connection with your True Self, your internal (eternal) reality. To do this requires determination, focus, and clear intention. The world of form is ever changing, so be prepared by getting strong in your purpose and do not waver.

Even when your endeavor is to promote self-love, the focus is primarily on physical form. (body shaping, eating healthy foods, facials, massages, etcetera.) Again, you are attempting to find the eternal through the temporal. Thereby inner peace is denied. You are mindful of thoughts about yourself, but you are not aware of your SELF.

This story typifies the problem. Notice the restless mind of the disciple. See if you
    identify with it.

There was a Zen Master walking along a mountain path with one of his disciplines. They happened on a cedar tree and sat beneath it to enjoy a simple lunch. The young disciple, having not found the key to mastery of silence, asked the question, *"Master, how do it enter Zen?"* (How do I enter the state of consciousness known as Zen – or Silence?) The Master remained silent for several minutes while his disciple anxiously awaited an answer.

The Master finally spoke: *Do you hear the sound of the mountain stream?* The disciple had been so preoccupied with his busy mind that he had not noticed the mountain stream. At once he began listening for the noise of the stream. He found this difficult, as his mind was not tuned to the sounds of nature. At last his thinking quieted enough for him to heighten his awareness to hear the stream. It was but a small murmur. *Yes, I hear it now.*

The Master said, *Enter Zen from there.*

In a while, the student started his restless thinking again. That which was *alert stillness* was obscured once again by mental chatter. *Master, I have been wondering. What would you have said if I had not been able to hear the mountain stream?*

The Master stopped and looking at his disciple said, *Enter Zen from there.* Thus, we find that entering the Silence or Zen can be done anywhere and at any time.

In the story, did you recognize the restless student who was preoccupied with questions and unable to sit in silence? He offers a metaphor for the undisciplined mind. It operates from a place of movement and physicality but has lost the skill to be still. Of course, as the master states, this can be corrected.

Entering Zen is the same as returning to our inner state of peace. As you can see by the story, mental discipline is required. The technique called meditation can supply that.

Meditation is a process by which you relax the body and conscious mind and move into the Inner Silence of Zen. Instead of giving heed to the endless mental chatter, you disciple yourself to listen deeply. Move to a deeper space. This heightened awareness offers the opportunity to reestablish your inner connection with spirit. Many people feel incapable of holding their attention on inner stillness. The ego's chaos, which is random chatter, rises from the mental program you were given as you were learning how to live in the world.

Chatter/mental clutter/inner static = programmed thoughts.

The chatter is an indication of engrossment in matter or form. Most make this mental noise their identification. That means the continuous flow of thoughts…. worry, fretting, remembering, second-guessing, what to do next - goes on incessantly and the person believes that it is who they are. It is much the same as believing their form or physicality is who they are. With external identification, there is no peace to be found because the superficial world and the mental chatter that goes with it are never static; it is ever changing. Neither is representative of who you are. The peace that resides deep within your consciousness is who you are. The key is to learn how to live *in* the world but not be *of* the world.

The baby exuded this consciousness or inner Light. He radiated to the world and he is happy. Perhaps it is time to rediscover that Light. Perhaps it is calling to you! With disciplined attention, you will find it again.

Activity

Thus, we begin by reconnecting to our uncluttered mind. Take a walk-in nature and "feel" each aspect - the wind as it flows through the trees and the earth as it squishes under your feet. Listen for the sounds of the birds, crickets, and insects. Notice each tree, flower and bush. Train your attention. Do this for a minute, then five and then ten. Build your tolerance to mental stillness and learn how to live by feeling your world rather than listening to constant mental chatter. In time you will experience healing from years of mental fragmentation. And in calmness you will become familiar with the vastness of Spirit. You will feel connected. It takes practice. Be steadfast in your practice every day.

***

Knowing is Power

To begin to develop inner stability and knowing, you must endeavor to see the big picture – in a sense, to become a visionary. If you were to stand on top of a ten-story building and look to the right and to the left, you would be able to note movement and activity. Perhaps you would see things about to happen.

For instance, if there was a car motoring down the street at a particular speed on the right side of the building and another car on an adjacent side doing the same thing, you might determine that, if everything remains as it is, these two cars will collide. By having this "higher" vision, you could signal one of the drivers to change speed and the potential collision is averted. That is what happens when we release our everyday, traditional focus and elevate the mind to "higher" vision.

Higher vision illuminates cause-effect relationships. It is not hard to recognize that if an abusive boss does not change his ways, eventually his brightest employees will leave to seek more welcoming ventures.

By the same token, as cause and effect is understood, anyone has the ability to alter the course of his life. That is what is meant by the edict *you reap what you sow*; you can always sow new seeds for prosperity, joy, health, and abundance. The potential to create a new life and a new way is unlimited, astounding and ever available.

Couple the awareness of cause and effect with understanding the law of possibilities, and you can surmise that possibilities abound. There are no limits. The field of possibilities is vast, unlimited. Striving for this expanded view of potentials is practical. It makes sense and offers incredible strategies and solutions and peace.

It works like this: The body is a vehicle and so is the mind. If we think of putting on a suit of clothes and then an overcoat, we have a metaphor for the principle of pure spirit entering the mind as a vehicle and then adding the body as an additional dense energy vehicle to be used for communication. We chose our clothes (beliefs) and we choose the overcoat (personality/attitude) we want to wear and express. These are the choices that set up the life pattern we live. (Remember, you can always change your clothes.)

When you perceive life from a heightened view, you are rarely surprised at the way events unfold. You can even listen to someone talk for a few minutes and predict his future. People are always setting up their lives by the way they think and the beliefs they hold and these are revealed as they express themselves. For example, when a person is fixated on an influenza epidemic or on a family trait of diabetes, you can be assured he will have the flu and develop diabetes. If a person is always frustrated because life doesn't seem to unfold the way he thinks is best, you can bet on his continued annoyance because he is unwilling to note the cause-effect scenario occurring. Frustration and need for control = more frustration. Of course, the opposite scenario is the individual who lives in gratitude for the many blessings that show up daily in his life. Gratitude = more blessings. As the great scientist, Albert Einstein said: *What you hold vibrationally in your mind, the Universe replicates. It is not a law of psychology or religion. It is a law of physics.*

Activity

At the end of the day, go through the occurrences of the day and ask yourself what the cause-effect relationship of each event was. Perhaps you were anxious driving to work and you managed to hit every red light and traffic jam. Anxiety = frustration = traffic jams. Or you felt alive and unbothered with the small inconveniences of life and you noticed people smiled at you and the sun was shining. Aliveness + peace = smiles of others and happiness for you.

Thus, even if you felt frustrated at the end of the day, can you pinpoint something that was wonderful – an event or person. Maybe you had the best latte ever. Perhaps you received a complement that you forgot to receive (revel in). Little by little begin to shift your attention to gratitude. It will pay off. Daily practice will yield enormous results. Your connection to higher consciousness comes through gratitude. The reason is that gratitude is a higher vibrational energy than frustration.

***

The Expansive Universe

Achieving the mastery of on-going connection requires expansion. The desire to grow is natural and aligned with universal substance. In other words, the universe is always expanding. (This has been proven scientifically.)

You are an integral part of this expanding universe. As you grow and understand more, you become more. You are learning to live in sync with your elemental or True Self. This is why people like Orville and Wilbur Wright, Thomas Alva Edison, Bill Gates, and Steve Jobs were driven to bring invention to the world. They grew by engaging their imaginations, curiosity, and technical skills and brought brilliance to the world in the form of invention and technology. They blessed everyone because they chose to pay heed to inspiration. Each of us has the same brilliance. We are uniquely designed to share our Light with the world.

Einstein said, *the important thing is not to stop questioning. Curiosity has its own reason for existence.*

If you were to drop the external pursuit of quotas, competition and comparisons, you are left with the spirit of freedom that urges you to peek into the next challenge and find place for your curiosity to discover what works and what doesn't. By opening your mind to potentials and ALLOWING, Spirit responds, and you are delivered insight, vision and even steps to bring magic to your endeavors.

This is the energy we were born with – a limitless imagination of possibilities that can take form as you give it life. Benjamin Franklin provides a great example of this drive for expression. Throughout his life he looked to the next step, the next invention, and ways to make life easier. Such was the case when he undertook the idea of harnessing electricity.

Franklin was gutsy when he stood in a field during a thunderstorm with a kite, wire, string, and key. He was testing his theory about electricity. He dared, even invited, lightning to travel down the wire and electrify the key. His goal was to find a way to control this power. He was brilliant and daring. Yet kept his experiment secret rather than chance being ridiculed, which tends to happen when people step out of their cultural box to explore new ways.

To be sure, Franklin's idea of harnessing electricity came through intuitively as all great inventions do. To go beyond the thinking mind, you enter a territory of deepest inspiration that only the curious can enter. It is intuition and it speaks to you in flashes and hunches. This is what drove Franklin and many others.

Franklin's ultimate effort was to improve life. To that end he asked himself a question every morning, *what good shall I do this day?* And as he completed his day his question was, *what good have I done today?*

Franklin's commitment to make life better, coupled with his courage, curiosity, and creativity, led to a number of cutting-edge inventions for his time. These include the Franklin stove, bifocals, the lightning rod, glass harmonica, and the beginnings of a storage battery.

What you want to remember is his boldness. Franklin had tremendous curiosity about how things work. He used this along with his desire to make life better as he delved into areas others would not consider. You might call him a spiritual adventurer. He was not interested in the status quo. He wanted more.

To develop the ability to go beyond everyday boundaries, we must cultivate the same desire to expand. We must want more. Self-confidence is born of curiosity and creativity.

As you evolve (unfold), you become undaunted by the opinions of others and your determination, like Franklin's, propels you forward no matter what. That is the adventure of life -

- inventiveness, curiosity, willingness to explore, and recording the results. It can be great fun. But the main thing is that as long as you are asking questions and seeking answers, you are growing.

Again, going back to the analogy of the ten-story building, you are looking out into the vast cosmos and higher mind. Intuition guides you toward possibilities. It is the still small voice that resounds in your mind. The one that says, *It will work. Try this.* And, just like Benjamin Franklin and others, you are given an idea, a solution, or your next step.

Activity

Record on a daily basis, what is your intuition (your still small voice) telling you? What are you being urged to do? It could be simple as taking a different route to work and then finding out the usual way was blocked with construction. Or you show up early to your job and find your boss is delighted to see you and has a special assignment that will further your career. As you record these intuitive impulses, you will discover your awareness increasing and nothing surprises you because you sensed it before it happened.

You will notice as you go through this book that there are many stories of people who *paid attention* to their inner nudges and were able to move forward in profound ways. Again, keep a record/journal and you will surprise yourself regarding the regularity of these occurrences.

***

Intuition – What it is and How it Works

Intuition cannot be explained scientifically because the very phenomenon is unscientific and irrational. In other words, can intuition be reduced to intellect? The answer is NO. Intuition is something, but it is not of the intellect. It comes from a deeper place where intellect is totally unaware.

The intellectual mind can *feel* it, but it cannot explain it and that is a problem for the intellect. The intellect (thinking, analytical mind) wants to disallow anything that cannot be rationally explained. Yet the intellect can *feel* the lap into intuition because there exists a gap. It knows that something has happened, but it cannot explain it because explanation requires causality. Intuition exists beyond causality as it emanates from a deeper, spiritual place. It just is.

Intuition is a different realm that is not related to the intellect at all. However, it can penetrate the intellect. The reason is that a higher reality can penetrate a lower reality, but not vice versa. Thus, your mind can penetrate your body, but your body cannot penetrate the mind.

That is why if you are desiring higher connection you have to release the body and mind both. Neither can penetrate the higher phenomenon of intuition. (That is why it is so important to spend time in the natural world because it is a world beyond intellect.)

Your physical being is gross, heavy, and dense and cannot rise or be lifted into higher consciousness. For this reason you have to let go of your body, your identity, and most of all your judgmental mind to move into the light energy of intuition or knowing.

You can get lost in thinking (intellect/chatter) and believe that what cannot be explained by the intellectual mind, does not exist. This keeps you trapped in thinking (and not feeling) and it disallows mystery and wonder to speak to you. This represents a narrow, closed existence that keeps you stuck (tethered) to a lower experience. And, as you disallow mystery, you also disallow intuition to speak to you. Again, Einstein proclaims, *the most beautiful experience we can have is the mysterious.*

A purely rational mind is closed within the boundaries of reasoning, which blocks intuition from entering. Yet, you can use your intellect without being closed to intuition. You do this by using reason (logic) as an instrument and maintain an open consciousness. You might say that you live in wonderment. You are open and receptive to higher energy and as it comes you *receive it.* This is what Franklin did when he logically tied kite, string, and key together to test out his intuitive theory of harnessing electricity.

When you are open to intuition, you can use intellect as an assist. It is a way of knowing that something has happened that is beyond me. This kind of receptivity will help you understand the gap.

The Gap

Let's consider the gap. An easy way to understand what is meant by the gap is to observe your breathing. Notice that when you breath in and before you exhale, there is a small interval /gap where no breathing is taking place. It is like a tiny rest period. The same is true when you exhale and before you inhale. Observe the space between the two. You will recognize a gap. This gap is a space of pure openness.

Notice also that there are gaps between thoughts. Practice slipping your attention into this gap. As you do that you will register a stillness. In time and with practice, you can expand your consciousness within this gap. That gives you an opportunity to experience pure consciousness without the contamination of thinking. It is also a way to connect with your quiet intuitive mind.

Intuition is a Direct Path to Manifestation .

Our Western Culture, in particular, has glorified thinking and intellectual attainment Yet, everyone has intuition. Many pay it no heed. That is a big mistake. You will find intuition to be the direct path to your desire. One way you can connect more strongly with intuition is to *feel* your environment. Wherever you are, sense the energy of that place, situation, or person. When you are at a meeting, sense the energy in the room - notice who is dominant and who offers no or low energy. Pay attention to who is fully present and who is just making an appearance.

It is important to observe energy while you keep analysis, thinking and opinions at bay. For instance, notice if your analytical mind wants to guide you. Example: This is a church, so it should feel like peace, etcetera. Ignore this input and allow yourself to be open and objective in sensing energy. It could be a church in deep organizational disarray, and peace is not to be found within its walls.

As you make *feeling* or *sensing* energy your practice, it will become a new habit and objective information will come easily. Doing this as a practice keeps your mind open without judgment or criticism. It is an exercise in creating mental spaciousness because you are eliminating the need to register judgments and opinions.

Alexia Briones VandeWalle followed her intuition on Jan. 7th, 2013. At the time, she was tidying her home and decided to call her mum. *There was no answer, and I heard clearly inside, 'She's taken pills. She needs your help'.* Alexia tried calling her two more times and her mum still did not respond. So, she jumped in a cab and raced to her mother's place. There she discovered that her unconscious mum had taken a box of benzodiazepines. Alexia quickly called an ambulance and her mum survived, but it was close.

There are many stories of people receiving intuitive flashes and rushing to the aid of a loved one. I have had similar experiences. When my inner voice was emphatic, and I moved quickly and averted disaster.

When these things happen, there is no question of what needs to be done. We follow our intuitive guide. And as things turn out, we are grateful for this voice.

If you are attentive and receptive, you will hear your intuition voice. There are times when you are guided to take a new route home from work and find out later that traffic was completely bogged down on the usual route. That is your intuition instructing. Or, you are urged to call a friend and find out that he really needed to talk to you.

A young lady was supporting her heartbroken friend as they spent the evening together. After dinner and coffee and then a drink, they decided to check out the dance hall. That is when she ran right into her future husband. Serendipity! Yes! That is how the Universe works.

The more we pay attention and listen to this inner nudge, the stronger we become. It is a fantastic, creative tool and worth every minute of time it takes to cultivate. Every art piece, architectural wonder, invention, and musical score came through its originator as intuition.

Franklin had the feeling that holding a kite and key in a thunderstorm would bring him closer to understanding electricity, and it did. Curiosity, determination, and courage are necessary.

You must be brave enough to symbolically hold the key in the thunderstorm. Making what some would call mistakes and taking bold steps is how you ultimately build trust in yourself and the Universe. It is in its truest sense relationship building.

You are opening a channel to your creative self. You are letting go of your left brain, follow-the-rules, traditional self to make room for your out-of-the-box, creative right brain. The channel is already there. Listening for it, following its guide strengthens it. You are literally moving away from the dominance of a small, conventional mind-set to expand to greater possibilities.

No matter what you require, it is available. You may not know how to get it, but your creative mind in connection to the universe does. Relax, listen, try new things and eventually you will happen across the exact right answer and the perfect solution.

When there is sincere desire and willingness to expand, you are always led to answers. Solutions and possibilities are continually offered. Perhaps not the ones you think you want, but they are available, nevertheless. Thus, a step to self-mastery and deep connection opens. In this way you experience life as a delicious adventure.

With each action you take, you understand more deeply that you are greater than the present moment. You are greater than the current experience and its outcome. And just by taking the next step, you have succeeded. Why have you succeeded? Because now you are bigger than you were when you started. Wow!

Activity

At the beginning of each day, ask yourself: *What good shall I do this day?* And at the end of each day, ask yourself, w*hat good have I done today?*

Keep a journal and date each entry. This allows you to go back and check your progress.

Make it your practice to notice energy wherever you happen to be. It will help you to journal your observations. Your daily log reinforces the idea of paying attention. When you do this you are practicing being present. Most people are not present in the moment in which they are living. They are fixated in the past or future and often completely miss what is going on now.

By practicing sensing (noticing, feeling) right now, you can easily slip into intuition and it will get stronger and you will note that ideas and solutions appearing effortlessly. All of this makes your life easier.

Additionally, play with the idea of entering the gap. Observe your breathing and notice the gap/opening between breaths. Then take a moment to mentally slip into the gap. For a second everything stops. It is another way to build the bridge to access higher consciousness. With practice, you will become good at taking momentary breaks in a meeting or at work by slipping into the gap. It is like taking a mini vacation from the busyness of the material world.

II. Knowing and Not Knowing

When you go into the space of nothingness, everything becomes known.

Buddha

How can one ever know anything if they are too busy thinking?

Buddha

Summary: There may be times when you pretend to know things you really don't to boost confidence and appear wise when, in fact, what you are really doing is increasing insecurities and losing touch with who you really are. You may resist learning for the same reason. It is possible that you believe knowing requires a degree of self-mastery, and it does. But accomplishment of this sort is achievable and does not depend on university degrees or awards. You have the intelligence to develop the qualities you need -- mental discipline, vision, and courage.

Shifting your focus to the heart will give you a completely different perspective and open the door to inner peace. Your goal of internal harmony is what you seek. Along those lines, there are moments when it is best to let go of your need to control outcomes and move yourself out of the way.

The idea of giving up goes contrary to our training. We are taught to effort through; never give up. Yet there are times when our attempts to control circumstances and people keep us from our goal. To say it another way, the universe has a better plan and we must we willing to give up our illusion of control and release our circumstances to a higher power. In this chapter I offer methods to facilitate this type of change.

***

When you lack confidence, the idea of being clear and knowing truth seems impossible. Yet if you consider the notion of formulating knowing by not knowing, at least you've found a map. If you are not feeling all that knowledgeable, the implications of having direction and a sense of knowing may seem outrageous. However, the truth is, in order to develop deep inner knowing, you must accept the state of not knowing. I know that sounds like an oxymoron or at least a Chinese puzzle, but it isn't because not knowing really does lead to knowing and I will tell you why.

Accepting that you do not know something is incredibly freeing. To admit you don't know the answer frees your mind from the ego's need to know everything. It places you in the open space of higher consciousness that has no requirement to impress anyone. Try it. Relax into *"I don't know."* Your gut might clench up, but your spirit will soar. *"I don't know"* sets you free from the pretense of knowing things you don't really know.

Your intellectual, egoic mind is limited to what you have learned in a literal, factual, linear way. Your not-knowing mind (intuition) has all the other answers. Admitting that you don't know something helps you achieve deep listening, which is imperative to connecting to higher consciousness. Not knowing is the state where creative impulse is born, and answers are delivered.

All great artists and inventors channeled this higher consciousness. This doesn't exclude great engineers, chemists, doctors, lawyers (all professionals). Their greatest ideas came through a higher state of mind. Often this occurred when they were most exhausted and could no longer *think*. It was at that point that they relaxed, and their consciousness was open enough to receive an answer they could not access before.

It happened to the great scientist, Marie Curie, a dedicated scientist in the field of atomic physics. She made history in 1903 when she became the first woman to receive the Nobel Prize in Physics. Her theory involved the discovery of polonium, radium and radioactivity.

As the story goes, Curie was stuck in her work while trying to solve a mathematical problem. She had tried everything and was totally exhausted and fed up. She appeared to be blocked in advancing her research. She finally succumbed and went to bed depleted. In her sleep that night, the conclusion she needed bubbled up in a dream. She woke up and wrote it down and then went back to sleep. The next day she checked it out her *dream answer* and it turned out to be the exact formulation she needed.

After that Curie sought to repeat this experience without success. She could not find the process or method because she was searching for it from her intellectual mind. The key for

Curie was to exhaust her conscious, reasoning, analytical mind so that her subconscious mind (intuition) could come forward with the needed answer. The deeper realm of subconsciousness is analogous to the vastness of the universe and therefore has access to all the answers we shall ever need. Currently scientists acknowledge that all great discoveries come forth from the deeper intuitive realm of mind.

The same technique works in your life. If you have ever bought a house, you understand it. After going through dozens of houses, you come up short. Nothing is right. Then, one day you venture down a street you didn't know existed and there you find the house you have been looking for.

Again, you exhaust your conscious, analytical mind and only then are you receptive to a new neighborhood, street, or section of town, and that is where your house has been sitting the whole time. You might say that you have to give up trying so hard. We humans have a credo that we can achieve anything if we work hard enough. Often the opposite is true. It is through giving up that you are able to relax enough to be guided. That is when your mind is open for new ways, ideas, and creative solutions.

This has happened to me on numerous occasions - in finding the right car to purchase, or house, office suite, and outfit for an event, or what to do next in business – you name it. It has happened to/for everyone.

Intuition happens to you – without any causality. Without following a path of what came before, it shows up. If there were a logical process to intuition, you could develop it like tuning to a particular station on the radio. But it is not a process and your best way of having control over intuition is to cultivate deep curiosity, wonder, and appreciation for all things natural. These qualities teach you how to be quiet and create mental space. Only then would you be able to "tune in" as needed.

The beauty of facing life unprepared I tremendous. Then life has a newness, a youth, then life has a flow and freshness. Then life has so many surprises. And when life has so many surprises, boredom never settles into you.

Osho

***

The Known and the Unknown

According to reason, there are two realms of existence, the known and the unknown. The unknown implies that which is not yet known but may someday be known.

Mysticism indicates that there are three realms: the known, the unknown, and the unknowable. Unknowable refers to that which can never be known. As it says in the Tao, *if you can define it, it is not the Tao.* (The all in all, infinity, the universe, God)

The intellect is involved with the known and the unknown, but not the unknowable.

Intuition works with the unknowable (with that which cannot be known). The unknowable will always exist as the unknowable and it is the realm of intuition. In other words, you can feel it, but you cannot define it or understand it. This sounds nonsensible but really means that which cannot be understood by our physical senses. The unknowable is the mystery and beauty of life.

It is the unknowable that provides life meaning.

Reason is an effort to know the unknown

And intuition is the happening of the unknowable. To penetrate the unknowable is possible,

But to explain it is not.

The feeling is possible, the explanation is not.

Osho

***

Instinct / Intellect / Intuition

We haven't talked about instinct yet, but it is important because many people confuse instinct with intuition, and they are not the same. Instinct is of the body – the dense self - and intuition is of the soul – the subtle. Between the two is the mind, the intellect, the expert, which never functions spontaneously. Intellect = knowledge and knowledge is not spontaneous. Instinct is deeper than intellect and intuition is higher than intellect. Both are good. Therefore, on a realm of higher to lower, it goes like this: Intuition (higher consciousness), intellect (knowledge), and instinct (of the body).

Intellect is the functioning of the head, instinct is the functioning of the body, and intuition is the functioning of your heart. And behind these three is your being, whose only quality is witnessing or observing. (Have you ever felt like you were looking out of two peep holes – eyes – into the dense world. If so, that was your being observing.

Your body functions instinctively. Your organs know how to function, your blood knows how to flow, and your lungs know how and when to breath. Physical functioning is instinctive. Hunger is instinctive. When your stomach growls because you haven't eaten for a while, your instinct is telling you to eat something. When you are dragging around out of exhaustion, your instinct is guiding you to sleep. Instinct is about keeping your body alive.

Everything that brings meaning to your life is intuitive (your heart). That means, survival, to exist, is without meaning. To live without a deeper sense of purpose has no merit. When you observe people with dead eyes, you know they are existing – but do they have purpose? But when you live out of your heart, you live aesthetically. You live from a higher realm. Art, music, beauty, love, friendship are emanations of the heart. The heart connects you to the Divine.

To live in a way that your head, your heart, and your body are a symphony is what you are meant to do. Then connecting to your greater being is easy. When these are conflicted, your life is a mess - wasted. The conflict is between instinct, intellect, and intuition. Harmony between head, heart, and body reveals the soul, your center. Living from your center is living in ecstasy.

As a therapist/coach, I see this conflict regularly. *I want to keep my job because it provides me with a lot of money, but there is no art to it, no inspiration.* This scenario is a conflict between head and heart (intellect and intuition). The head is trapped in structure (the material world) and the heart wants a higher purpose. The heart yearns for a way to express the depth and beauty of the soul and the head (intellect/egoic self) wants to be safe. Many people trade the song in their heart (what they truly want/need to express) for what they assume to be safety. (Keeping the body alive.) Of course, safety of this variety is never really safe because as you cut out the creativity of your soul that yearns expression, you begin to wither and die. You cease to live from the inside (soul) out. In time, the physical body succumbs as well and physical death follows.

Mahatma Gandhi said it well: *The enemy is fear. We think it is hate, but it is fear.* The spiritual master, Patanjali, said, *"when you are inspired by some great purpose, some extraordinary project, all your thoughts break their bounds, your mind transcends limitation, your consciousness expands in every direction, and you find yourself in a new , great, wonderful world."*

***

Your Mind as a House

Get to know the house in which you live. Gurdjieff used the metaphor of the house to describe consciousness. This is the house in which you live. *Man is a three-story house. The first story is the unconscious, the second story is the conscious, the third story is the super consciousness (highest expression of mind). When there is no repression within the mind, you become human* (fully alive) *for the first time. In other words, you have moved out of the animal kingdom. This is absolutely necessary if you want to know truth and really understand yourself as a spiritual being.*

You are operating in all levels of this house/mind at all times but where you put your focus in most important. If you keep your attention on the first floor, unconscious mind, you are operating unconsciously (instinctively). If you live out of your intellect / second floor (what you have been taught), you are limited. When your focus is on the superconscious mind, you are free and open to highest intelligence (intuition). Whatever you need to know if available to you by remaining open in an unknowing state.

Currently scientists confirm that all great discoveries are intuitive, not intellectual, meaning they all come forth from the deeper realm of mind. You can learn to tune in to this level in much the same way as you tune a radio to a specific frequency. To do this requires focus and willingness to listen.

History informs us that inventor, Thomas Alva Edison, developed the light bulb after thousands of experiments to find the right filament. Edison was undaunted, in his work and he always knew that eventually he would discover exactly what was needed. He also knew that he didn't have to depend solely on his intellect to find these answers. He had another technique.

When Edison was stuck in his process of engineering a new invention, he would take a nap on the cot in his laboratory. His method was to hold a steel ball in his hand when he laid down for a nap. As his body relaxed, his hand would release the steel ball and it would hit the floor with a loud bang. The noise woke Edison and he would register his thoughts on awakening. It was his practice that whatever thought he held in his mind when he woke, would be the answer he needed to his current riddle. He credited his intuitive mind in supplying many of the answers he sought.

This same method of accessing higher mind also works in your life and doesn't even require a nap. It is about relaxing with an open mind and allowing the answer to appear. Edison would program his mind to present his answer on awakening. You can do the same thing.

If you have ever bought a house, you understand it. After going through dozens of houses, you come up short. Nothing is right. Then, one day you venture down a street you didn't know existed and there you find the house you have been looking for. Thus, you exhaust your conscious, analytical mind and only then are you receptive to a new neighborhood, street, or section of town, and that is where your house has been sitting the whole time. You might say that you have to give up trying so hard. We humans have a tendency to believe that if we work hard, we will achieve what we want. Sometimes you have to let go while keeping your mind open.

This has happened to me on numerous occasions - in finding the right strategy in business, right car to purchase, house, office suite, or outfit for an event – you name it. The same thing has occurred to/for everyone. And, it is repeatable process.

Activity

Have fun with this exercise. Here it is: Admit that you don't know. When someone asks for directions and you don't know the way, say (with gusto), *I don't have a clue!* When you are asked what is going on in the world – *I don't know.* What is the weather supposed to be like – *I have no idea.* Who won the football game*? Don't know!* Where is the colander? *What's a colander – don't know.* Are you having fun yet – you can know the answer to this.

The idea is to notice how it feels to enter "not-knowing." Does it give you space to just be? It is a relief to not have to know everything. Does it give you a break from your ego? Practice this exercise for a month before you draw conclusions because it might take that long for your ego to give up resistance to not knowing. But trust me, it will be good for your psyche.

Second activity

Practice programming your mind to have an answer you need before taking a nap. Then have pencil and paper ready when you wake. Don't do yes or no questions but challenge your mind with real needs and solutions. In time you will get this method down and it will prove to be helpful in all areas of your life.

A variation of this method would be to take a drive and when you have returned home you will know what you are to do. Or after a meeting I will know. Or after the party I will know. You get het point.

***

Develop the Art of Not Knowing – Next step

For most of us, the unknown is both friend and foe. At times, it can be a source of paralyzing fear, and at other times it can be a starting point where adventure, creativity, and transformation begin. How we relate to the unknown is a key element in personal growth and healing ego wounds. Its mystery forms a deep current that runs throughout all spiritual and mystical traditions.

In the martial arts, there is a condition known as *not knowing*. It works like this: When you are in a competition with an opponent and do not know what he will do next, you clear your mind and remain open. You place your focus on *feeling* the energy of your opponent. In this open state, you connect with him energetically and sense his energy. Basically, you bond with him. Consequently, as he plans to strike you with his right hand, you are feeling the thought as he thinks it. You move as one being and shift your body to avoid the strike. It becomes a dance of openness, waiting for the next move. With practice, your ability to dance in this energy is refined and strong.

It is in this same manner that we develop our greater vision. Instead of an opponent, we open to the universe and feel the pull and push of energy. When we agree to not know, we open our minds to knowing from a deeper level. We sense when things are happening. We sense movement and others' intentions.

The knowing we develop over time is vast. We view, from the top of the mountain, so to speak. Sensing universal energy is what happens when birds leave an area prior to an earthquake or tsunami. They feel a shift in energy and know to take flight. You can do the same thing. Of course, you will walk and not fly.

To move into not knowing, you must become centered and open the slate of your mind. You must strive for emptiness, like a cup ready to be filled. There can be no agendas or boundaries. Your mind must be quiet and ready to receive. Think of playing a game of baseball and you know the outfielder is going to throw you the ball, but you are not sure when or how hard. You are focused and open, ready to receive the ball. The same thing works in life only you practice this skill of openness every day and all the time. *I am ready to dance with the universe. I am open to the energy flow in my life. I am paying attention.*

Consider for a moment that mental stability is soft and open. When you are still, you are ready to ask for and receive higher information. In stillness, you are able to *feel* and inwardly *hear*. It is a matter of mental training. You can learn how to be still with nothing in front, behind, or left or right. As you train your attention, you develop the ability to stay completely in the moment without past or future.

Many people don't have tolerance to not know. It is frightening to them. They are dependent on the noise of the ego and the clutter of busyness to stay distracted. They want to believe that they can set their own plan and agenda, and things will go accordingly. They use the chaos and conflict of the superficial world to occupy their thinking and avoid inner space. Yet, setting aside the external world is the way we learn to communicate with our inner world and ignite our intuition. It is the way to develop real peace and true understanding.

Activity

Pay attention to silence. This could be to walk outside in the evening and listen to the silence of nature. Notice the sky, moon, and stars. They know what to do without prompting. Notice the scurry of animals. They are being led by the stillness of vulnerability. Just stop and notice. Try to immerse into nature and become one with it.

Then notice the rhythm of your breath and the space between the inhalation and the exhalation and exhalation and inhalation. Observe the rhythm and with each breath you will gently move into stillness. It is this practice that connects you to your Source. Nature grows in silence; babies gestate in silence. Life moves in silence. Be still and know that I am God – silence.

Activity

Every day spend time in silence. Close the door to your office and sit quietly for 15-30 minutes. The best way to do this is to go out in nature. Be still and FEEL nature. Let your mind build up tolerance to stillness. It will ultimately pay huge dividends in bringing peace and stability to your life.

***

Tips on Developing Intuition – It is all about paying Attention

Intuition, we all have it. Some use it daily and others don't. Do you listen to your head or your heart? Head = intellect; heart = intuition (deeper knowing).

Intuition can show up as feelings, a great idea, a symbol presented in your life (a sign, a person, an animal, or even a situation). In fact, everything, when viewed from your higher mind, has significance and everything is a symbol of some sort. All can be used to guide your growth.

Recently I was returning home from a spiritual retreat. As my friend and I drove we spotted a vulture just ahead, sitting in the middle of the road. It seemed to be waiting for us. As we approached, the vulture spread its wings and floated aloft. It appeared to be conveying the ease of flight.

When I looked up the symbolism of *vulture*, purification and rebirth, it seemed to convey perfectly the theme and intent of the retreat. My friend and I were indeed feeling a sense of release (purification) and rebirth into a new state of being / consciousness. The vulture was an affirmation for our work.

Dr. Bernie Siegel acknowledged that *there are symbols everywhere.* Buckminster Fuller, the developer of the geodesic dome, said that the *Universe is speaking to us all the time, we must learn to listen.* He was referring to the symbols that show up in abundance.

Symbols show up as animals (vulture), feathers, songs, weather (sudden storm, dark clouds, etcetera), and invitations (events, parties, to meeting someone). There are even symbols in what appears to be tragedy and hardship. We may be shown that it is time to move on, correct an emotional entanglement, or make an adjustment in some way.

Jesus lived in higher consciousness. He instructed his followers, *"You shall know them by their works."* He said works, not *words.* Often we get confused because people say one thing and do another. A radical example would be the fellow who says *I love you* and then smacks you. Words say one thing; actions state a totally different reality. A person is completely out of integrity when his words and actions don't match, and you are out of integrity if you believe him.

My suggestion is that you ignore what people say and pay close attention to what they do. Is this person kind to the little people – waitresses, cab driver, and store clerks? Actions reveal the person. When we pay attention, we begin to observe life rather than be entangled in it. The more we observe without judgment (just watch it like a movie), the more we can cultivate a deeper sense of

intuition. Why? Because we are no longer distracted with
intellectual illusions.

Once we become entangled with people or situation and make
judgments, feign outrage, become attached, we lose our edge. That
means we are distracted from the still, small voice that resides
within the heart. That is a heavy price to pay.

The truth is that love is action, not words. It is amazing to me
how people want to be told how much they are loved when their
friend or partner is going out of his/her way to show them.

Can you see? In this confused state, we put words above
actions and misjudge our situation.

Yes, we are operating from our head and not our heart.

One of the first steps in strengthening your intuition is to
FEEL. That means feel the situation you are in, sense the person you
are with, notice the energy in a situation. FEEL it. As you move
beyond your intellectual (head) self, you will find your feeling sense
will prove a valuable ally guiding you to your right answers and
direction.

Many people ignore their feelings and that is a BAD mistake.
Your feeling sense is to be trusted but it must be in the moment.
That means that if you had a terrible experience with a tall

Italian man in your past and now you react badly to all tall,
Italian men, that is not your intuition speaking to you, but a past
memory. It may take time to sort out memories versus true gut
sensations. Yet with practice, this can be done.

Practice FEELING and be willing to be wrong, because for
sure your intellect will try to interfere. Nevertheless, practice makes
perfect.

When Jesus healed the blind man, the Pharisees (who
represent the "letter of the law," follow-the-rules mentality –
rational but not intuitive) challenged him and said you must be a
devil (evil) because you did something out of the ordinary and you
had the nerve to help this guy on the Sabbath – a time of rest. In
other words, you broke the religious law of the time and that makes
you *bad.* These Pharisaical thoughts, and everyone has them, are
not spiritual or intuitive. They represent the way we have been
indoctrinated. Our narrow beliefs in how things *should* be.

It so concerned the Pharisees that Jesus healed on the Sabbath
that they wanted to get rid of him, stone him. Think about it… you
do a kind act – do you second-guess yourself – maybe they won't

appreciate it, maybe I gave too much or too little, perhaps they won't understand, or I may have overstepped the boundaries, yada, yada, yada. This second-guessing is Pharisaical. These are the thoughts that talk you out of living spontaneously, spiritually, and with love. They are based in egoic (intellectual) materialism in that they attempt to convince you to rationalize who you are instead of striving to feel the deepest compassion, love and kindness that you are and to operate from that.

If you were listening to your deep love (heart) what would you do today? Can you do it without second-guessing? Can you do it now?

There are different levels of intuition. Some guide you from past experiences as mentioned above – *watch out for the tall Italian guy*. This is the result of an imagined threat and is more instinctive than intuitive. Then there are deeper levels of intuitive knowing that help you cultivate your highest essence.

To access these profound levels, you must become non-judgmental, non-attached to specific outcomes, and non-resistant to what is. If you have not developed these qualities, then that is the next work to do.

Parting thought: Whatever work you do to strengthen your intuitive understanding will bring you tremendous rewards. As you move your awareness to deeper, more profound levels, you glean peace, joy, wisdom, health, abundance, and knowing. These are the greatest rewards you could ever want. And, unlike money, you can take these qualities with you when you move on to your next experience.

***

Mental Training - Moving to the Heart

The whole idea of not having control over emotional reactions is a misnomer. Of course, we have control. We are always choosing. We do not have to be vulnerable to what we have reacted to in the past. We don't have to succumb to anger, resentment, or depression when faced with challenging events. But we do have to train our minds and have forethought to alter old pathways and take ownership.

To believe that the world controls your feelings and reactions is giving up and living in hopelessness. It means that if someone gets sick, loses a job, or has a negative exchange with another, he has to be depressed or upset. It means that in order to be happy, everything has to go the way we want with no bumps in the road. That is ludicrous.

If we accept these ideas, we have completely underestimated ourselves. We are way bigger than caving into primal reactions and our challenge is to strengthen resolve and train to manage our mental and emotional state.

The change is to become non-reactive. We take a moment and choose to look deeper at what is really happening and we determine another way.

Start with intention. If, for instance, you choose to be peaceful, then that must become your dominant thought and resolve. You must commit to it. You must choose peace over and over, even when stressors appear to taunt you. This is not about denying emotions but seeking higher energy.

Emotions trace back to beliefs (thoughts). Much of the time we have been trained with illogical, irrational beliefs that cause us to feel out of control. We feel crazed because we attempt to manage outer circumstances rather than our reactions to them. We can affect ourselves, and, in fact, we are required to do so, but we cannot rule the external world.

Start by observing your reaction to an event, comment, or person, and trace it back to a mental construct that you have accepted as truth. For instance, if you believe that everyone should (or must) get along and you notice people who are fighting, you will have an emotional reaction – anger, upset, sadness. Why - because fighting goes against your idea of peaceful cohabitation.

Another example might be the ideal that everyone should be polite or considerate of each other and when you witness those who do not follow that edict, you become irate, upset. Why – because your belief has been violated. Again, you are focused on what you cannot control, other people, rather than what you can – yourself.

Of course, there are positive emotional reactions as well. You notice kindness or generosity and find it sweet and compelling and react in a joyful manner. The same thing is true. The belief that kindness is good + an observed act of kindness = positive emotional reaction. It is fortunate you get to experience a joyful event. Yet the basic premise is to decide what you choose as your own condition of emotional stability and stay true to it.

Day to day we have thousands of opportunities to observe and react to events and people and there will be many that don't agree with our values and beliefs. People being unkind, critical, angry, resentful are but a few stressors that can evoke emotional reactions.

The truth is that we are ever experiencing a world of myriad possibilities. We get to choose how we want to operate with these varied interactions, career situations, relationships, family members, technology, schedules, daily tasks, everything. Before we turn our nervous systems to mush, we want to develop techniques to manage our state of mind.

Thoughts have energy and so do emotions. When we have a thought, energy is instantaneously transferred to the emotional body and then the physical body. That is why we feel them in our bodies. As we manage our thoughts, we also affect our emotions and our neurology, chemistry and musculature. In fact, we are managing our health.

Stressful reactions are draining. They rob of us of energy and joy. But as decision makers, we can learn to adapt to challenges and stressors and remain peaceful. It is about maintaining an on-going state of peace and objectivity.

Often people will wait until they are alone or in a quiet place or on a retreat to re-group and de-stress. But that is the same as shutting the barn door after the horse has escaped. We need methods to re-set ourselves before the damage is done.

After experiencing a tense moment, you feel drained, and need to re-collect the emotional, mental, and physical energy lost to your system. You can learn to do this quickly, with least damage. Mental mastery involves being in the moment and managing your business as it occurs. If you don't learn how to do this, you can easily accumulate degenerative effects on the body, nervous system, and mind.

What I refer to is the ability to step back in the moment. To pause when things get tense is a matter of training and discipline. Just as a martial arts master observes before acting, you do the same thing. Hesitating a moment to give yourself time to decide what to do conserves a lot of energy and preserves health. You can ultimately use this energy to be creative, have fun, and live a fulfilled life. You can be peaceful when all around you are falling apart. Again, it is a choice.

Can you remember a time when you changed your attitude toward a person or situation, and everything turned out better than you expected?

See what you think of this story: It is about a 24-year-old boy who was gazing from the train's window and shouting to his dad, *Look, the trees are going behind.*

A couple sitting nearby felt pity for the young man's childish behavior. The young man's dad just smiled. *Wow, look Dad, the clouds are running with us.*

At last, the couple could not resist and leaned forward to ask the father if he had taken his son to a good doctor. The father smiled and said, *"Oh yes, I did that, and we are now returning from the hospital. My son has been blind from birth and he just got his eyes today."*

This is a story where you could easily assume one thing and after gaining more information, your judgment changes on a dime. You might start with annoyance, shift to humility, and then gratitude. I chose this story to illustrate the fact that you can radically change your view of things, if you give yourself a moment to process your thoughts and feelings.

Continuing on with our process. Take a moment to record some events in your life where you quickly changed your perceptions and adopted a different attitude. Perhaps you thought someone was aloof and unfriendly and then you found out he just lost a loved one and is grieving. As you remember a few of these moments, they will remind you that judging too quickly is a mistake.

Next think of a time(s) when you were peaceful, relaxed, and happy. Photograph one or two of these moments in your mind for future reference. You want to be able to recall these at a moment's notice. Remember the feelings that accompany these memories. Example: you are sitting on the beach watching the waves roll into shore and you feel peaceful and awestruck at the beauty and power of the ocean. Or, you are holding your child while he/she sleeps peacefully, and you are filled with comfort and gratitude. You get the idea.

Activity

Here is the step-by-step process to practice. Remember, practice makes perfect. When a demanding circumstance occurs – you are stuck in traffic, the boss is in a bad mood – step back, place attention on your heart (the center of the being) and breath. Then quickly go back to the peaceful or happy memory or someone you love. Keep your attention there. Do not budge. All of this is accomplished in seconds.

Your heart is your love center. Your heart energy is love, nurturing, kindness, and wisdom. When you move from head to heart, you immediately change perception. So, the steps are:

1) Recognize the stressful feeling
2) Shift focus (step back) and move to the heart
3) Breathe and remember someone or something you love or a happy memory – FEEL it.
4) If speech is necessary, speak honestly from your heart.

Here are times to practice: business meetings, in line at the grocery store, in traffic, late for a meeting, at the restaurant, at work, with your family and every other challenging situation and all the time. Soon peace will become your dominant energy and focal point and you have achieved mental-emotional stability.

***

Giving Up and Letting Go

Have you ever felt you reached the end of your rope and there was no place to go? Often that is the very state you must get to in order to make room for the answers you need to show up. Or to say it another way, when you are totally befuddled and confused, maybe even exhausted, that is when letting go and allowing your creative mind to click in makes sense.

A man was chased off a cliff by a tiger. He fell and just managed to grab a branch and hold tight. Six feet above him stood the tiger snarling greedily. A hundred feet below, a violet sea lashed against fierce looking rocks. Then to his horror, he noticed that the branch he was clutching was being gnawed at its roots by a rat. Seeing he was doomed, he cried out, *O Lord, save me!* And he heard a Voice reply, *Of course, I will save you. But first you have to let go of the branch.*

Thus, we come to the purpose of this section – sometimes you have to give up and that means let go of the branch, the judgment, the job, relationship, the investment, or anything else. When this is the right protocol, we hear an inner voice that urges us to *let go!* I follow with stories to illustrate the point.

Perseverance and belief truly are analogous to success. 19th century physicist, Marie Curie, stated, *Life is not easy for any of us; but what of that? We must have perseverance and above all confidence in ourselves. We must believe that we are gifted for something, and that this thing, at whatever cost, must be attained.*

Marie Curie made history in 1903 when she became the first woman to receive the Nobel Prize in Physics. As a dedicated scientist, Curie developed the field of atomic physics. She theorized on atomic structure, and discovered polonium, radium and radioactivity.

Later in 1911 she received her second Nobel Prize. During World War I she championed the use of the portable X-ray machine, taking them to the battlefield. As a result, Curie is credited with saving many wounded men, as well as numerous who suffered various longsuffering infirmities.

Her story would most likely have had a different ending if it had not been for the answer that was presented in her dream allowing her to move forward on her theories and formulas. As the story goes, Curie was stuck in her work trying to solve a mathematical problem. She had tried everything and was totally exhausted and fed up. She was apparently blocked in advancing her research. She finally went to bed depleted. In her sleep that night, the conclusion she needed bubbled up in a dream. She woke up and wrote it down and then went back to sleep. The next day she checked it out. It turned out to be the exact formulation she needed.

After that Curie sought to repeat her experience without success. She could not find the process or method in her research because it wasn't there. The answer came because she gave up and opened to the deeper, intuitive mind and it provided the solution.

The key for Curie was to exhaust her conscious, reasoning mind so that her subconscious mind could come forward with the needed answer. The deeper realm of subconsciousness is analogous to the vastness of the universe and therefore has access to all the solutions we shall ever need. Currently scientists confirm that all great discoveries are intuitive, not intellectual, meaning they all come forth from this deeper realm of mind.

The same technique works in your life. If you have ever bought a house, you understand it. After going through dozens of houses, you come up short. Nothing is right. Then, one day you venture down a street you didn't know existed and there you find the house you have been seeking. Again, you exhaust your conscious, analytical mind and only then are you receptive to a new neighborhood, street, or section of town, and that is where your house has been sitting the whole time. You might say that you have to give up trying so hard. We humans have a tendency to believe that if we work hard, we will achieve what we want. Yet working hard is not always the answer. Sometimes you have to give up while remaining mentally open.

This has happened to me on numerous occasions - in determining strategies for business, finding the right car to purchase, house, office suite, and outfit for an event – you name it. It has happened to/for everyone…even you!

The process is to try all the conventional methods and finally give up. Then when your mind is exhausted with all that doesn't work, you become open to accepting the thing that does. That is when you notice the thing you didn't see before, or you venture into a new store or part of town and voila! There it is. It was always there, but you couldn't see it because your mind was cluttered with how it *should* look, where it *should* be, and how it *should* happen.

The key is to remain open and allow the answer to come. In Marie Curie's case it came in a dream. It can come in a variety of ways. One of my clients was in a bookstore and a book dropped on her head three times before she realized she was being given a message. And, yes, it was the book she needed. Try it and see for yourself.

Another client was looking at property to purchase when a hawk landed right in front of her and she knew that she was to buy this property. The hawk was a symbol of broad vision and it represented a message from her intuitive mind. Thus, messages and intuition show up in various ways. Sometimes you turn on the radio or television, or open a book, and what you needed to know is right in front of you.

Quite famous in his day, American scientist Elmer R. Gates (1859-1923) was a virtuoso inventor. He had a unique method of inventing called psycho-taxis.

First, he experienced through each of his senses all the sensory data on the subject at hand. In brief, he would categorize data using sensory input. Then he recreated each sensation in order over and over. As he repeated this recollection, the blood flow to the particular area of the brain where the data was processed increased. This process brought into dominance the neurological structures where subconscious connections are made. The result was new insight into the subject.

Gates researched mental processes. His insight was that there were efficient ways of using the mind that led to greater mental capacities - not merely more original ideas, but to concepts that were more frequently and completely true. He approached his study with zeal, and enthusiasm that *"knew no bounds and acknowledged no difficulties."*

The short version of his process was that Gates would sit in a quiet room for hours waiting for the answers he needed in reference to the issue he was working with. This is how he invented the foam fire extinguisher, an improved electric iron, and a climate-controlling air conditioner.

He was also productive in the fields of X-ray, alloy casting, electrically operated looms, magnetic separation devices for mining, and an electronic music synthesizer. So basically, he knew no bounds and acknowledged no difficulty. He *knew* the answers existed and he was willing to wait for them. He stayed open and they were presented. What would happen if you knew no bounds and acknowledged no difficulties?

The point then is even when you are mentally exhausted and see no way to accomplish the goal you seek; the mind is still full of options and possibilities. Sometimes we just have to give up – let go – surrender – before we receive the answer or solution, we're after. What do you need to let go of now? This could be an irrelevant method, irrational belief, relationships that are not enriching, a job that has fulfilled its purpose or even material things that are no longer useful or bring joy. When you let go, you create space for something or someone better to enter your life. There has to be space for that to happen.

Activity:

Pick an area of your life – an issue at work or in your relationships where you are not sure what to do and relinquish it to the greater universe. Do it like this: *I am clueless about how to deal with this. I know there is a solution, so I am handing this to you. I know that you will present the right answer to me. I am grateful. Thank you! (Yes, this is like a prayer, but then all thoughts are basically prayers.)*

Then hand it over and forget about it for now. When the solution appears, note how it comes – a random comment, a passage in a book, a bright idea, something you see on television, a dream. Who knows? Enjoy the process.

III– Commitment

We spend our lives, all of us, waiting for the great day, the great battle, or the deed of power. But that external consummation is not given to many: nor is it necessary. So long as our being is tensed, directed with passion, toward that which is the spirit of all things, then that spirit will emerge from our own hidden, nameless effort.

Pierre Teilhard de Chardin

Set a Clear Intention

Summary: Setting a clear, focused commitment is the key to all accomplishments – invention, solutions, revelations, and advancements. If you fear the word "commitment" you might have good reason. Perhaps you don't want to be stuck in a promise that turns out badly, so you resolve to avoid these pledges. If so, you are probably missing the point because every commitment you make is to yourself. Each one moves you in the direction of the life you desire. Your mind is a powerful dynamo of energy. The moment you set a clear intention, everything in the universe shifts to make that objective a reality. Learn how to set a powerful intention and step back ready to respond to opportunities that show up. Each intention takes you on a journey to self-improvement, which culminates in the fruition of your desire.

***

The key is to develop conviction. Absolute certainty has no bounds. It sets your course and establishes your destiny. To be precise, set your intention unequivocally.

Jesus told his disciples to say to the mountain, *Go throw yourself into the sea and do not doubt but believe it has been done.* That is conviction.

Champion Tennis player, Andre Agassi declared, *When I won Wimbledon, I had played that match over and over again in my mind and saw myself being handed the trophy.* He used visualization as a power tool to maintain his clear intention. He held his vision and it was made manifest. It worked for him and it will work for you too.

When you set a clear intention (to know something, to be something, or to obtain something) your mind develops laser focus. Magical things happen when you are clear as to what you want. The mind has the ability to mold mental substance (like play dough) to coincide and emulate your desire. Think of it as a kind of shape shifting.

I knew a man who grew up in a housing project. His family was poor and as a child, he regularly stole food in order to eat. Being hungry was a strong motivator for him because it led him to vow that he would do whatever was necessary so he would never be hungry again. This commitment directed him to a business education and an executive position in a large international delivery service. Because he was determined and committed. he took appropriate action and pursued the opportunities that showed themselves until he achieved his objective. And he never visited hunger again.

It is interesting to note that there is a device in your brain near the Medulla Oblongata called the Reticular Activating Sensor or Device. Its function is to alert you to opportunities that match your desire or intention. It is called RAS for short. So that once you set a clear intention, your brain nudges you when an opportunity shows up to fulfill your intention. Often, you will have a "feeling" about someone or maybe an event you should attend. By following up with this feeling, you find yourself in the exact right place with the exact right person to satisfy your intention. Here is an example of how it has worked in my life.

Once I made a list of all the places I wanted to travel, and I put in the criteria that each trip would be either free or inexpensive. Then I let go and turned it over to the universe. I literally stepped back to see what might happen. I was clear in my intention – I wanted to travel and do it with little or no money!

Within a ten-month period, I was offered three free trips – steamboat Springs, Colorado; Hilton Head, South Carolina; Williamsburg, Virginia, and an inexpensive trip to Cabo San Lucas, Mexico. Excellent! Had I not made this list, I may have passed on these opportunities or they may not have even shown up in my life. But as each was presented, I was clear that the universe was complying with my stated desire. Of course, the same process works for you.

Once you establish a clear intention, you enter a timeline, which resolves in achieving your purpose. Even a slight shift in your intention (you change your mind or admit self-doubt) will alter the course of this timeline and you end up in a totally different place than you had originally intended.

Think of it this way, if a ship makes a small navigational deviation in its course, perhaps one degree, in the long term it will end up thousands of miles distant from where it would have harbored had it stayed with the original navigation.

Thus, we conclude that with every intention set and every adjustment made we are engineering big changes in our thinking and our lives. That is what self-mastery is all about and that is what brings us to deep connection to our True Self and the dynamic power of the mind. With commitment you discover your path and when you stay true to it, you arrive right where you need to be. It always works.

What do you want out of life? What changes are you willing to make to achieve it? What actions make sense right now?

Activity

1) Write out a goal list. These don't have to be major goals like having a million dollars but can include a few of those. Perhaps there are things on this list that you want to experience or own. Perhaps even an adventure you desire. There may also be immediate items to achieve right away.

Next, read over this list morning and evening and spend a few minutes feeling each of these items as though it has already been completed or manifested in your life. See and feel the new car in the driveway and the smile of new car ownership. Imagine yourself walking into a job situation where you are welcomed and appreciated. Feel the applause generated with every victory or win. Now, put the list aside – your intention has been set. When a relevant idea or opportunity shows up, follow up and do what is necessary.

1) Set an intention to connect with your deepest spiritual self. Feel this connection as peace, happiness, and knowing. Realize that by setting this intention you are making a commitment to yourself to be guided and to

listen to the voice of intuition. Each day take note of
how this guidance showed up. It could be a nudge to
call a friend or make contact with someone you haven't
seen for a long time or investigate a travel destination
or new job.

Once I was in an office supply store waiting to be served. A
young man also waiting his turn decided to help me even though he
didn't work at the store. He noticed me being ignored and his sense
of customer service was offended. So, he decided to help me get the
numbers of the items I wanted to order and wrote them down on a
paper to hand to the clerk at the store.

As we discussed my requirements for office furniture, I
noticed that he was getting his resume printed. I asked him what
kind of work he was seeking and offered to share his resume with
anyone I knew who might need his help. At the time I worked with
various business owners and they often needed help, especially from
a go-getter enthusiastic, out-going fellow who wanted to be in
service.

The next day I was reading his resume and noted that his work
history perfectly matched someone I knew who owned a metal
fabrication business. I called this person and he was so understaffed
that he was working on his own factory line. When I mentioned this
young fellow and his work credentials, I was told to "*send him right
over.*"

In this instance, I did my part in making the call. So did the
young man who showed up, and the business owner opened the
door to a potential employee. The balance lay in matching the
needs of the machine shop owner and the qualifications of the
young man.

My intention was to help some good people connect. The
young man wanted to work in a business where he could provide
good service and have time off with his family. The business owner
wanted dependable, skilled, willing, enthusiastic employees.
Everyone was clear in his intention.

Knowing what you want, being clear, setting an intention, and
doing what is in front of you to do yields results. It always yields
results. Setting a clear intention to make the connection to your
Greater Self will yield results as well.

Second Activity

Decide what you want in the area of health, abundance, relationships, service, work, and creative expression. Be clear. State each intention as a positive. In other words, instead of inferring, *I don't want to struggle*, you are clear that your intention is to live with ease where answers are supplied, and you follow through with clear action and purpose. If or when you forget what you want, go back to this list and read it over or reframe it. Clarity of intention is key to achieving your desires. A clear intention would be stated as *I choose to live a life of free flow and abundance.*

***

Dedication and Discipline

Many people consider discipline to be a kind of punishment. Yet that could not be farther from the truth. Dedication and discipline actually free you.

All successful people are disciplined. They all maintain self-restraint, consistency, and a sense of order. That means they set a goal and they move toward it with unrelenting, focused attention and action. This was true of British Prime Minister, Winston Churchill, during WWII when he declared that Britain will NEVER surrender to the Nazis.

Lee Iacocca, former CEO of Chrysler, was highly disciplined when he pulled the Chrysler company out of bankruptcy. During that time, he was inventive to go before congress to ask for help in saving the company, and congress complied. Then there were Presidents John F Kennedy and Franklin D Roosevelt, both of whom held high views of what could be accomplished and pushed forward with firm resolve to fulfill their visions.

In his book, **Managing the White House**, Richard Johnson described them in this way.

If they didn't like the pastries on the tray, they proceeded into the kitchen and baked a few original pastries. (Of course, this is a metaphor. Yet it described the unrelenting spirit of these men to eliminate all options that compromise their values.)

That is the type of determination needed to advance spiritually. We often think that persistence relates only to material goals, but it just as important to apply it to spiritual goals. If you have a desire to achieve highest consciousness, or strong intuition, or to connect with your deepest self, you will need a disciplined approach. This means setting aside time daily to meditate and do the exercises outlined in this book.

Once a commitment to do the work has been made, the next step is setting up your schedule to make sure you have the time and energy to do the work. What that means is that you become firm in your resolve to practice the exercises and techniques outlined in this book. You must also be on guard with the personal ego. It loves to distract your efforts toward control. It will offer many stories to capture your attention and keep you mired in the material world. Self-discipline will keep you focused on your bigger prize and it will help you proceed with deliberate action to take control.

Managing the mind is what it is all about. It takes time to formulate the life and person you want to be. This formulation can only succeed in a focused, nurturing mental environment.

It is the same way a baby flourishes in a peaceful, harmonious home.

If living in highest consciousness is what you want, then create the proper mental environment to foster your desire. If your ego steps in as a spoiled child demanding attention and attempts to direct your focus away from your goal with negativity or drama, disconnect from it. (Place your attention elsewhere.) It is like setting a cup on the table. You place your ego to the side and ignore it.

Your need is to grow in discipline and control so that you may discover the unlimited nature of your mind and the deeper connection to your soul that is ever available. Your life can be one of unending miracles as you grasp the connection to your spiritual essence. It is a treasure that forever gives.

When Jesus said to keep your 'I' single and all else shall be given unto you. He was referring to the discipline of maintaining strong focus on the goal of living as a spiritual being in highest consciousness. When you have succeeding in knowing who you are in this way, you shall be free indeed. Plus, you have on-going access to highest intelligence, answers, solutions and knowing.

IV. Making the Connection

The choice is yours. You hold the tiller. You can steer the course you choose in the direction of where you want to be— today, tomorrow, or in a distant time to come.

Clement Stone

Dwell on the beauty of life. Watch the stars and see yourself running with them.

Marcus Aurelius, *Meditations*

Summary: In this section we explore various methods to strengthen your intuitive connection. Stepping into vastness, finding your natural, universal rhythm, learning how to entrain to higher consciousness and identify quantitatively with the universal field of energy we call God are techniques that work. Through these various practices we strengthen our identification with our center of love. It is through love that all things are possible – all connections are made, tangible or intangible.

The truth is that vastness is your true state. In this section you are instructed on how to connect to the vastness of your true self. In so doing, you shift your identification to universal consciousness where everything is known, and all things are possible. Other techniques to strengthen your ability to stay in this expanded state, increase your potential to be guided by higher intelligence.

***

Focus in Vast Spiritual Energy

It can be a bit overwhelming to recognize the vast energy in which we live, breath, and have our being. Yet, learning how to step into this massive energy field is both freeing and empowering. The reason for this is that vastness *is* your natural state.

In this section you are encouraged to step away from identification with your small physical being and "thinking" mind to realize the vastness of your true self. As you do this, you are shifting your identity to universal consciousness where everything is known, and all things are possible. Strengthening your ability to stay in this expanded state increases your intuitive ability and potential to be guided by Higher Intelligence.

An ocean wave appears for a moment and then it is gone. It is just a temporary form, appearing out of a constant: the ocean. The ocean is ever-present. The wave is for a moment. The on-going, continuing reality is the ocean, not the transitory form of the wave. The ocean always exists. When it is active, you see the waves, and when the ocean is silent, there are no waves.

Either way, the ocean is the reality. The constant. It remains.

Individuals appear like waves, each having characteristics. Some are big and others small. Some are violent and others subtle. One rises to life while another dies. Yet, the reality behind each wave (individual) is the same.

Each wave may appear as separate, but deep down, it is identical. It is connected, as every wave is produced from and composed of the same ocean.

A person dies and another is born. How can they be connected? One wave dies and a new wave rises by gathering energy from the dissipating wave. The dying wave may be helping the new wave rise. The dispersing wave may be the cause behind the rising one. Deep down, they are composed of the same substance. Whether big or small, violent or subtle, they are related. As individuals we influence others. Sometimes we support and advise them. Often we educate and nurture them. Our energy is ever present in the same way as the ocean supplies substance for the creation of the next wave.

What seems to be individuality is really illusion. Each person is but a tiny form appearing from the vast ocean of Universal Consciousness. Each one rises and falls within this quantum energy and the unified field remains. The duality that appears to be a wave and an ocean is not so. We are the same, waves in a cosmic ocean. Non-duality, or oneness, is the truth.

We have the opportunity to view ourselves as individuals or to focus deeper to the commonality of Spirit. We reside in a vast ocean of Spirit, each individual demonstrating different characteristics, strengths, and weaknesses. When we connect with the deep energy and truth, our true selves, we are as vast as the ocean, and just as powerful.

Everything we need, we already have. We can relax into Spirit and recognize our magnificence. This is the truth of who we are. It is how we connect to all that is.

To go deeper into the self and the vastness of being, accept that you are alive in an unlimited field of energy. To do this shut your eyes and close down your sensory perceptions – hearing, seeing, touch, smell, taste. Be quiet in the present moment and watch your breath go in and out in its natural rhythm. Stay with this awareness for a while ... a few minutes. Notice that as you observe your breath, your awareness broadens, and you can sense an inner spaciousness. With practice, you will become quite comfortable in this stillness and will be able to open even more to the vastness of this field of energy.

Quantum Physicists acknowledge this field as the Unified Field, Quantum Field, or Holographic Field of energy. Theologians refer to it as God. Whatever name you choose to give it, it is the energy in which we live, breath, and have our being.

Inner stillness introduces this new reality. You can surrender to it and merge with it. It is not something you fathom intellectually. You have to experience it - *feel* it. This quantum field is in you and around you and everywhere - omniscient, omnipresent, omnipotent. Floating in it is analogous to swimming in a vast ocean. And it is peaceful.

You can experience this vast energy by entering it. To practice, stand in an open field and imagine your mind stretching to take up the entire terrain. Or another method is to imagine being at the top of a mountain and looking out over an expansive territory. As you gaze, you allow yourself to expand into the scene, the clouds, the grass, the trees, and rocks. You open your energy to embrace everything. It is what yogis refer to as being as small as an ant or as vast as an elephant. You let your mind expand to vastness.

Maybe you have merged with a melody and rhythm of music you love, where your sense of self disappeared into the ocean of sounds. Or you may have inhaled a smell so delicious, perhaps your favorite dish when you were really hungry, that you disappeared into the aroma.

Perhaps you have sat by a river, conscious of its steady flow and trickle, and entered into stillness. Possibly, you have been so in love, your heart lifted and lightened. Each of these experiences is an entrance to vastness.

To expand into vastness, you must stabilize in your center. In other words, focus your attention on your center. You can feel it. Usually, this is an area around the solar plexus. As you connect with your center, you are free to feel the energy around you. All athletes do this. Observe great athletes and you will see that they operate from a strong center. This gives them the ability to move with grace and agility.

Becoming centered is important if you want to experience vastness. You can do this before meditation so that you are leaving behind your small physical self in order to be the entire ocean or the vast sky. It is freedom.

Developing this skill of entering vastness gives you the opportunity to know beyond intellect and sensory perception. In vastness you connect to ALL energy, every person, the meaning behind events, and the guidance you desire. You are no longer looking at the surface of things; you are understanding *why.*

Sanjita Singh's story speaks of vastness because Sanjita had to let go of a dream of being a cardiologist in order to move into the limitlessness of a new life. She was highly motivated to become a cardiologist until she was diagnosed with an autoimmune disease, which led to her being confined to bed for almost three months. During that time, she occupied herself by writing sad poems.

When Sanjita heard the doctor inform her parents that medicines weren't working to improve her health, she was heart broken. Slowly and sadly, she let her dream of becoming a doctor evaporate. She had become a sad poet because she could barely move or talk, but she could write. After three months, a miracle happened. She began to show signs of recovery. She could walk a bit and she felt hungry and thirsty. Soon, she recuperated. Her pre-med schoolmates, however, had already gone ahead in their studies while Sanjita was left behind with no goal or aim in life.

She decided to join a Bachelor of Arts program. Then she went on for a master's degree where she found poetry inspiring. During that program, she wrote hundreds of poems, both sad and romantic. At the end of her master's studies, she took top honors.

She followed her poetry with articles and got selected as student editor of her college magazine. Her goal had changed from being a doctor to having her bylines read. This thrilled her. Then she found a job as a copy editor and correspondent for one of the leading daily newspapers and has never looked back.

Sanjita originally felt that she would be a failure if she could not serve people as a doctor. But now, she realizes she can serve by being the voice for others. She believes that life is the biggest teacher and guides us in the most graceful manner. It is our assignment to be patient as we grow in understanding and to stay strong as we move ahead.

Sanjita is an example of moving out of the restrictive belief that we have the best plans for life. Allowing the universe to guide you into the vast possibilities available leads to discovering happiness.

What dreams and goals have you needed to leave behind? In what way and by what means is this vast field of energy we call the universe guiding you now? Are you flowing with it?

Activity

Pick one of the vastness experiences mentioned (standing before a vast field, on top of a mountain, or before the night sky) and practice using your imagination to expand your energy accordingly. Do this for five to ten minutes a day and note the changes you experience in your body, in your mind, and in your interactions with others. Notice the sense of freedom and observe when answers and solutions come more quickly to you. Definitely keep a journal to track your progress.

***

Find the Rhythm

There is a cycle to life, a recognizable on-off rhythm. It is easy to note this rhythm in nature. Trees and foliage exhume stillness. Animals stop and listen and let Spirit be their guide.

When man goes with this current, he experiences a sense of rhythm and rightness, perhaps centeredness. When he forces action, he (we) experience strain and struggle. Constantly doing things and going places is a form of resistance. Ironically, pushing and forcing action may seem more comfortable because it is a familiar thing to do. (We live in an action-oriented world.) Yet, there is a payment for living in stress and out of natural rhythm.

We can learn to recognize when we are forcing movement and decide instead to default to our natural pace and rhythm. You do not see a tree hurrying to grow, a flower rushing to bloom, or a baby frantic to crawl. Each move in its own rhythm and progress is made, yet there is no stress. Study these rhythms and you will discover you have a rhythm too. Notice your breathing and heartbeat. Notice the rhythm of your gait. Are you rushing? What rhythm feels most natural?

Finding your rhythm and remaining centered in Spirit will eventually and with practice lead to honoring your timing. This may be a first step in complete self-acceptance.

Ambiguity often breeds anxiety. This unease can drive us to search for new ways and directions to resolve what seems to be the problem. Yet through discipline, this kind of vagueness can be endured. It is a learned skill. Uncertainty passes when it is time to act or take a new direction. As you remain centered in Spirit, you will always find your way.

***

Fear of Failure

Most people avoid meditation because they *think* of it as work. They also fear that they won't do it perfectly. They don't know how to quiet their minds. They have trained for so long to hold a busy, chaotic mind; thus, meditation seems impossible, even scary. They fear failure.

There are also folks who fear what they will discover from meditation, maybe that they are not good enough. They may project their fear of unworthiness on to God and believe that they will be judged harshly as they move into this inner rarified energy. Actually, they are the ones judging themselves harshly because God is love and does not judge.

Learning to quiet the fear-based mind trains you to make love your center. Love, the opposite of fear, houses no accusations, judgments, or doubts. Love can guide you to deep rest from confusion. And you discover along the way that fear is a contrived mental construct – an illusion. Quieting the mind helps you move beyond fear and see the absurdity of it. There are many mental constructs (beliefs) that are absurd. This could be your chance to recognize them!

What if you don't have to meditate perfectly? What if there is no such thing as perfect meditation? What if you find out that you are beautiful and loved? What if you don't have to do it at all? What if you can simply rest and let go and God will do the rest?

Activity

Pay attention. Check in with your body several times a day and ask, *what do I feel right now? What do I need right now?* You might discover that answers come easily or maybe not. Be patient and still. Perhaps it is time to take a break or make a particular phone call. It could be that instead of grabbing a sandwich on the run, sitting quietly and breathing feels better. Or, maybe you need to stand up, drink water, and walk around the room. As you check in, you will discover that finding your rhythm is easier than you think, and it is an important step in connecting deeply with your intuitive mind.

***

Use Entrainment

Often people are miserable because they have bought into ideas and values that don't work. Yet they continue to rationalize that it is the right way. If this is you, you have been entrained to false images and it is time to figure it out.

People are continuously immersed in images and words that dictate how they *should* express in the world. Buying into these concepts restricts you with false values and limitation. Everyone does not have to be pencil thin and a millionaire by the time they reach thirty. You must discover your own values and live by them. By understanding the principle of entrainment, you acquire the ability to focus on what is important and release everything that doesn't fit.

Entrain means *to board or put aboard a train*. We can become entrained or board the train of other people's choosing if we are not careful. For instance, everyone is raised in a certain cultural environment and can become entrained to those habits, rituals, or belief systems even if they don't make sense. We can *buy in* without even knowing it. Have you been taught ideas that don't feel right and seem illogical?

Entrainment can also be defined as the synchronization of individuals to a certain rhythm. This is called brainwave entrainment. We all know that children learn their ABCs by using the rhythm of a song. "A B C D E F G – H I J K L M N O P – Q R S – T U V, etc." When the child forgets the alphabet, the song helps his memory click in. Educators use this method to teach math and linguistics as well. You may remember this verse:

30 days has September, April, June, and November
All the rest have 31
Except the second month alone with 28,
until leap years gives it 29.

Can you hear the rhythm in your mind as you read these words? Advertisers use the principle of entrainment in their commercials.

A smile and a coke. (Coca Cola)
Everything is good at Hoods. (household items for rehabbing)
We're here because you like nice things. (furniture store)

Here is the Oscar Mayer jingle:
My bologna has a first name, it's O-S-C-A-R
My bologna has a second name, it's M-A-Y-E-R
Oh, I love to eat it every day,
If you ask me why I'll say,
Cause Oscar Mayer has a way with B-O-L-O-G-N-A

This process of entrainment has also been illustrated by hanging two or more clocks on a wall in close proximity. Each clock has a different time setting. Within hours, the most dominant clock will have entrained the other clocks to register its time. The same thing is true of dominant people. If you don't have a strong sense of self, you can easily become entrained by another's dominant personality and beliefs – even if they feel wrong.

There is a story about an American Indian who found an eagle's egg and placed it into the nest of a prairie chicken. The eaglet hatched with the brood of chicks and grew up with them.

Throughout its life, the changeling eagle thought it was a prairie chicken, scratching in the dirt for seeds and insects to eat. It clucked and cackled and flew no more than a few feet off the ground in a brief thrashing of its wings with a flurry of feathers, following the flock's example.

After years pass, the changeling eagle grew very old. One day he viewed a magnificent bird flying majestically far above in the sun-lit sky. It floated gracefully on the powerful wind currents scarcely moving its golden wings.

What a beautiful bird!" What is it? inquired the changeling.

That is an eagle – the chief among birds. But don't give it another thought for you could never be like him, spoke his neighbor.

And the Changing did not give it a second thought and he died believing he was a prairie chicken.

That is a sad story of entrainment. No doubt you get the point. YOU are the one to decide if you are a magnificent creature who can soar through life creating whatever magic you choose or a limit-filled being of little imagination and drive.

Don't let your flock define your life adventure. That is your call. Entrain instead to the vastness of who you are. Spend time imagining the great things that are possible and the magnificent people who routinely perform miracles and you will be one of them.

Here is another story of entrainment with a happier ending.

Monterey, California is a coast town and for many years, a pelican's paradise. As the fishing boats came into harbor and they began cleaning their catch and the fishermen would fling the offal to the pelicans. The birds grew fat and lazy and, eventually, when the offal was utilized for other things, the food supply for the pelicans dried up.

When this change occurred, the pelicans made no effort to find their own fish. They had become used to waiting around for others to feed them. Soon they were gaunt and thin and some starved to death. They had forgotten how to fish for themselves.

You might say that was the end for the pelicans, but not so because an inventive person found a solution to the problem. New pelicans were imported from the south. These birds were accustomed to foraging for themselves and they were placed among the starving pelicans. The newcomers immediately started catching fish. In a short time, the hungry pelicans followed suit and the famine was over. Once again, the dominant pelicans entrained the starving birds and their natural instincts were restored.

So, you get the idea that a dominant energy can entrain a less dominate energy. You can be the dominant energy in your life. You decide what you allow in your mind. That is taking control. It is self-mastery!

Realize also that there are predictable effects when you choose to hang out with a crowd of naysayers. Unless you push yourself to become the dominant personality, you can easily relinquish your mental conditioning to negativity. People do this all the time and they have lots of great excuses for yielding.

I've known Susan, Beth, or Josie my whole life or *that person is my family, I was raised with them.* This means that the excuser does not put his best interests ahead of the cultural ritual of family gatherings or kindergarten acquaintances. Nor does he set boundaries as to what he will discuss or the amount of time he will spend with these groups.

Ultimately, to achieve self-mastery, you must be attentive as to what you automatically yield to and the habits you have cultivated that divert you from your intention or goal and change them accordingly.

You can also see how someone like Nazi leader, Adolph Hitler, with his loud, blustery countenance and his vision of a great nation could entrain a whole population into performing outrageous acts. The German people's desire was to come out of the loss and humiliation they experienced in World War I and gain some semblance of power. He worked this desire and entrained them with his vision of power and in the process destroyed millions.

Unfortunately, this phenomenon occurs every day. Watch television news and you will see it. Observe the commercials for prescription drugs or diet pills and you will see it. Who is the most dominant person in your family or at work? What control do you observe? Who have you let dominate your views of the world?

We can use the principle of entrainment in positive ways to achieve deep connection with

Spirit. Study great leaders (Jesus, Buddha, Mahatma Gandhi, Nelson Mandela, Bishop Desmond Tutu, The Dalai Lama, Mother Theresa, Wayne Dyer, Oprah Winfrey) and notice their mannerisms and style. Choose people you aspire to be like and mimic them. In this way, you can keep your energy high and focused on a bigger picture and greater possibilities. Choose wrongly and you have accepted smallness.

Always question: Does this make sense to me? If you question yourself, you will be led to "right-thinking." This means that intuitively you know what is the highest and best path for you and you can learn to live it. Make sure your environment reflects the intention you set. There are great people everywhere. They are the ones that entrain to higher values and beliefs.

Have you become entrained into an image? It can be Joan of Arc, Martin Luther King Jr., Fidel Castro, Bozo the Clown, the shy kid in class or the bully. Choose the image. Your mind will move to your dominant image and your dominant goals. When you become convicted on an end result your mind will draw on its resources and the universe and you shall have it.

Consider an evolved being… his Light, his countenance, his peace and wisdom. What would it feel like to possess such energy? How can I hold this image and move gracefully into its fulfillment? Can I let this be my dominant energy and desire?

Activity:

Step one: Create a jingle in your mind that you repeat over and over. *Every day in every way I get better and better. The universe is my Source. I am ever abundant. No matter what, the universe has my back.* These are examples of phrases you can use. A lady I knew repeated the phrase: *Health, joy, abundance* throughout the day. It kept her on track. Pick a phrase that can become your internal mantra and entrain your mind to hold it as your truth. If and when you lose focus, bring yourself back to your mantra.

Step two: Find one or two people you can use as symbols for the kind of life you wish to exemplify. Study them and remember their characteristics each day. Reflect on how they think and live and use their actions as templates for your own.

My examples have been leaders like Nelson Mandela, Bishop Desmond Tutu, and the Dalai Lama for their courage to maintain their values and stand up to challenge in the midst of great conflict. They are inspirations to me. I love their energy.

***

Think God

Practicing the Presence of God is just that, experiencing the Presence of ever-present, ever-available Spirit. All you have to do is think *God* and that's it. No other action is necessary. It is a form of focusing your mind and remembering. Remember your best friend in grade school? Remember the prom or your first boyfriend or girlfriend? Remembering God is like this. God is a Presence, like air. We don't think about air and we forget about God. When we remember God or remember air, both are everywhere present. Both are ordinary and miraculous at the same time.

Think of a fish swimming in the ocean and looking for water. That seems ridiculous. It is the same for us *looking* for God. We are in God. God is everywhere all the time.

Another phrase we use for taking a break is *quiet time.* The only action is to *take* the time. The quiet does the rest. In the Bible, it is written to *Come into the Kingdom as a child.* It means to live your life in openness, receptivity, innocence, and playfulness. Children rest and play. They don't work hard. Rest and play can be foreign concepts regarding connection and spirituality. However, if we peek into the lives of great spiritual leaders, we discover that they are grounded in those principles.

Here is an experiment. It is not official but suggested! Take five minutes to breathe before you start your day. Sit quietly and observe the breath going in and out of your body. Notice the breath. Notice if it has a texture or temperature. Observe it as energy. You can even ascribe a quality to the in-breath, such as energy, light, joy, and ascribe another quality to the out-breath, such as stress, worry, or fatigue. Just take these few minutes to rest in Spirit and find your center. It will provide huge benefits throughout the day. There are more exercises below.

Because we live in a busy, often driven, chaotic world, spirituality can be thought of as one more item to add to the schedule. Yet, being *spiritual* is an attribute to insert on the list of *personals*, rather than to your *To Do* list. We often try so hard to be everything that the effort gets in the way and ends up blocking movement instead of enhancing it.

This week expand your concept of what spirituality includes…especially a little more breathing space and some quiet time. Here are some suggestions to help make it easier. Enjoy!

- Instead of listening to a meditation CD, put on a great Broadway musical.
- Go to a comedy club or a funny movie instead of viewing something educational and politically correct.
- Read a great mystery or novel instead of a self-help book.
- Instead of getting up an hour earlier, sleep an hour later or go to bed an hour earlier.
- Instead of adding more to your *To Do* list, try taking some things off it. In other words, tackle less. Lower your standards.
- Let God work on you instead of you working on God.

Yes, rest is a spiritual experience. It is elegant, extravagant, joyful, and replenishing. It prepares the mind to connect deeply with your spiritual essence. God is love and love is who we are. As you think God, you feel love.

Activity

Take a break - play!

***

Move to Your Center to Become Love

The moment you have in your heart this extraordinary thing called love and feel the depth, the delight, the ecstasy of it, you will discover that for you the world is transformed.

Krishnamurti

A wonderful lead-in to this chapter on love is a Sport Illustrated "kids of the year" story. The story features the Long brothers and they offer a supreme example of the power of love.

Conner and Cayden Long were celebrated at a star-studded event in New York City. The event itself was to honor Miami Heat Star LeBron James and there were a lot of celebrities present such as Jay-Z, Beyonce, and Duke University coach, Mike Kryzewski. Yet the light shown most brightly on Conner's and Cayden's accomplishments. Here is their story:

Cayden suffers from cerebral palsy but that is no hindrance for Conner because he includes his brother in all his sports. The two compete together in triathlons with Conner pulling Cayden behind him in a raft during the swimming leg, towing him behind his bike during the cycling portion, and pushing him during the run. The brothers love coming together for these triathlons, and they inspire everyone that watches or hears about them.

Motivated by the Long's story, Coach K told Conner and Cayden that they have scholarships to Duke waiting for them when they get older. LeBron said that he is supplying a private plane for the brothers to go from their Tennessee home to Miami, to meet "the guys."

Even Jay-Z and Beyonce wanted to shake hands with Connor and Cayden.

The Long brothers illustrate what love is really about. When you love someone, you don't care what condition they are in, you just love them. Connor didn't deal with his brother as a disabled being. He saw him as his partner and companion. He saw him as a complete being.

That is the nature of love.

The story of the Long brothers is a great introduction to achieving a deeper understanding about love. Conner saw Cayden as his beloved brother. He did not consider him less than what he was, his best friend and companion. He did not register a burden or a problem. He saw through the eyes of love and because of that he discovered ways to include his brother in his activities. Love made this doable.

In this section, we examine the opportunity to BECOME LOVE. That means you give up resistance or contraction and open to the deeper, natural you, which is expansion. As the personal self seems to disappear (opinions, judgments, concern about appearances, stories), a new reality of greater love emerges, which allows you to be fully connected to Spirit. At your core what you really are is LOVE. As you let go of the hindrances and blockages, you begin to *feel* this truth and live fully as the energy of love. Peace and expansion then become your experience.

When you embrace your true nature, which is love, the opposite emotions cannot come into you. An example of this would be that when a room is filled with a bright light, there is no darkness. Darkness cannot enter. Whereas, if you dim the lights, darkness can enter the room. That is to say that when you are not in a state of real love, the other darker emotions can take over. Yet, when you are brimming with love, there is no room or space for other feelings to enter your mind. It is as easy as accepting people for who they are... period!

Most people have a great need for attention and approval. It is because they feel insecure and insignificant. Identification with the body form evokes the belief in limitation and scarcity. The body is small and limited and has many requirements – food, rest, and movement. To shift attention beyond the material body to the larger energy that comprises who you are, evokes identification with the greatness of your True Self. You are love; you are Spirit; you are exalted energy. By staying your attention on these truths, nothing else deters.

***

The There is an energy center in your body, which is known as the heart center. It is the place where pure love is expressed. This center gets shut down and locked when you seek attention, approval, affirmation, and external attention to the exclusion of giving to others.

There is a reason for that. We are designed to express or give our energy and talents away. We project energy in our efforts - creating, nurturing, kindness, helpfulness, thoughtfulness, etcetera. It can be through repairing things, cooking, writing, helping, nursing, computing, accounting, lawyering, or a million other things. But when energy is held back and not expressed outwardly by serving, helping, or giving it away, the natural process is reversed. It is reversed when you try to "get" or draw energy in, from others, to fill your imagined need for adulation and attention.

By reversing the natural energy flow, you actually become unloving. Often, we see this dilemma in people who assume to be entitled. They take a stance that the world owes them. In so doing, they forget to gift others with love and support. The result is misery.

Your heart center is open when you express unconditional love toward others. At these times it radiates with overflowing, energizing energy and support. This is your natural state.

You also experience greatest health when you are giving love to others.

The metaphor would be the sun. The sun radiates outward. It is constantly sending energy (sunlight) to the universe. If it were to reverse this direction, the universe would shut down. Thus, it is the same with you.

You are designed to radiate love. When you shift into a "getting" mode, you reverse the natural current of energy in your body. That is not to say you are not to receive love. *Receiving* and *getting* are two different things. Receiving is as natural as giving whereas "getting" is aggressive and unnatural.

It takes courage to go deep inside and love. When you venture deeply into any emotion, only that emotion remains and the personal you ceases to exist. That is total giving.

When you are expressing (radiating) deep love, you may even experience a momentary feeling of 'you' disappearing for a few seconds. As you work on being intense and total in everything, this experience of the egoic or personal you disappearing happens more often and for longer periods. As you cease spending time as a personal self, you are mastering the art of being love. At that point, you are operating from a deeper state, the True Self, the reality of love! This is when you become independent of the external world. This doesn't mean that your body dies. It means you exist more fully on a deeper level of life. It is living life fully and eternally. It is my belief that great masters live in this exalted state. In this condition you have full access to the field of all possibilities and the answers and solutions you require. You are connected.

In the same way, when you are brimming with love and you aren't distracted by the needs of a personal self, all problems disappear, and you feel only love. All the pain, shame, guilt, resentment, anger, and fear that used to be part of your mental make-up are gone. You literally become the radiance of love.

By the same token, when people concentrate on anger, they become anger. When they focus totally on resentment, they become resentment. The heat of anger or resentment ends up destroying them. It is a choice that projects or translates into an experience.

There is a story about a fellow who knew how to love. It centers on a blind girl who hated herself because she was blind. She also hated everyone else except her loving boyfriend. He was always present for her and loved her deeply. She told him that if she could only see the world, she would marry him.

One day someone donated a pair of eyes to her and she was able to see everything including her boyfriend. For his part, he said that now that you are able to see the world, will you marry me? But the girl was shocked when she saw her boyfriend because he was blind. As a result, she refused to marry him.

The boyfriend walked away heart-broken and in tears, and later wrote a letter to her saying, *just take care of my eyes, dear. I will always love you.*

This story expresses love's dedication and commitment. It does not mean that if you are unable to give up your eyes, you love less. Yet you could approximate that through his actions.

This fellow became love and even though his girlfriend was unable to reciprocate, his love opened him to the highest field of awareness.

By moving into a total experience of love, you begin to feel a sense of responsibility for a much larger family than your own personal family. You begin to extend to humanity at large, a family millions of times bigger than your own. This is yet another indication of the personal self-disappearing. As the personal egoic self dissolves, the greater, intuitive Self (Higher Self) becomes your dominant being.

The more responsibility you take up, the more you expand. Responsibility is something that can be easily shrugged. But if you don't dismiss it and keep on shouldering it, you will expand, and divine energy automatically flows in you.

You can recognize this phenomenon in great leaders. Again, the examples of Mohandas Gandhi, the Dalai Lama and Mother Theresa are obvious. Each took on great responsibility to bring Light to the world and ease suffering. They appear almost transparent because they were operating at a higher level of awareness and love than the general populace. They have become icons as vehicles of divine love channeling through for the benefit of the greater whole.

Only when you feel this overflowing energy flowing in and through you can you take on more and more responsibility and touch lives. As it grows, you will naturally be drawn to take action to remedy the maladies around you.

If you look deeply at your life, you will discover that this evolution of love is the reason you have been placed in certain situations. You are there to recognize the needs of the many so that you can bring your talents and love to bear in helping and serving. When you move into love, you stop seeking attention and approval and become a source of energy yourself. You cannot experience this reality with your mind, only with your heart.

When you become love, you melt the ego. Earlier your ego was rigid, and solid, and you felt separate from others. But when your ego dissolves, you feel like you are losing your separate identity and that is good, and freeing, and it is deeply connecting.

It is good because you exist beyond names, form, position, status and things. Thus, what you are losing is nothing except the illusion of what you are NOT. You are not your name, your body, or house, job, or family. You need to lose the illusion, in order to expand into what you are. You are Light, Spirit, Joy, Boundless Energy. That is what is meant by the edict that you must lose yourself in order to find yourself. You lose the small self (ego) so that you can gain your True Self – love.

The center of your Being is totally silent. This center is your true nature --the actual YOU. You have sought to find yourself in all sorts of places, situations, relationships and people. You have looked outward, into the world, not inward. Now the only place to look is within.

***

Someone Who Found His Purpose in Love

Here is a story about a person who became love. Scott Neeson was a Hollywood mogul who lived a Hollywood lifestyle as president of Twentieth Century Fox International. He was set to start a new position at Sony Pictures International when he decided to take a five-week hiatus to cleanse himself from his years in the film business. Because of his passion for Buddhist monuments, he embarked on a tour of Southeast Asia and India to tour monuments and that is when his life changed forever.

While in Cambodia, Neeson asked to see the worst poverty in the country. As he remembers, *they took me to Steung Meanchey, a garbage dump, a hundred yards deep and covering twenty-five acres.* As he entered the dump, his perspective on life completely changed. There he stood looking out over hundreds of children scavenging among the garbage, searching for food. The temperature was more than 100 degrees Fahrenheit, which meant that the decomposing garbage was producing methane gas and the ground was essentially as hot as molten lava or, in this case, molten garbage and the stench was unbearable.

Parents who could not care for their children due to debt, illness, alcoholism or remarriage abandoned them on the dump. It was a horrendous sight.

Neeson felt drawn to help but had a prejudice against charities, as he felt most of the money donated did not go to the ones who needed it. Yet, it was clear that he could not ignore these children.

He knew that the children he saw would live and die in this dump. Or they would be taken for trafficking. As he contemplated this dilemma, a nine-year-old girl walked past him. She was in a wretched state completely swathed in rags to protect her from the violent heat and because she had no place to leave her clothes, she wore them all. Her eyes were all that showed.

Through the skills of an interpreter, Scott Neeson learned that the girl was there with her mother and sister. Quickly he used his ability to strategize and solve problems and found a place for the family to live. He made arrangements for the girl to go to school and her younger sister, who was sick with typhoid, to be admitted to the hospital.   He also put together a system whereby he could send money from Los Angeles to their mother each week.

Within 90 minutes and $35 a month Neeson had profoundly changed the destiny of this family. Plus, it was clear to him that as a human being, these children were his problem. Neeson was hooked by the mere fact of how easy it was to alter a child's life.

When he returned to Los Angeles, he could not forget the Phnom Penh garbage dump. The urge to help more children got louder for him. For the next year he made monthly trip to further the cause, getting more children involved, and hiring a staff. He naively thought he could live between the glamorous world of Hollywood making a million dollars or more a year and continue sending money to Cambodia.

What I didn't count on was the emotional trauma of moving between the indulgent lifestyle and then within twenty-four hours, standing in probably the most squalid, impoverished place in the world, where children and mothers are dying in front of you for lack of simple medical care. Having those two worlds come together was something I couldn't live with.

His clarifying moment came when he stood with four sick children under ten years of age that belonged to no one. They were dying because no one was able to take them to the hospital. At that same instant a well-known actor called Neeson on his cell phone upset because his private plane was not stocked with the proper amenities. Suddenly all the anxiety about giving up his job to live in Cambodia disappeared. This irate, spoiled celebrity served as his clear signal that he was on the right path. When Neeson returned to Los Angeles, he resigned amidst much criticism that he was making a disastrous choice to give up his dream job. But as Neeson put it, *I didn't want it anymore.*

Neeson sold everything – his boat, house, cars, everything - and moved to Cambodia and started the *Cambodian Children's Fund* in 2004. He works with impoverished communities centered around the former garbage dump at Steung Meanchey by providing programs in education, leadership, community outreach, health care, childcare, and vocational training.

The CCF provides education that will take the student as far as their abilities allow. So, if they put in the hours and pass, they can go all the way through university. The fund supports them all the way. They also assist the whole family by supplying benefits. If the child goes to school, the parents get free health care at a medical clinic and are offered an opportunity to refinance their debt. They help families start small businesses or buy back the family land.

As Scott Neeson puts it, *I've never had so little and so much at the same time. I have virtually nothing in the way of material possessions. Strangely, there's nothing I need. It's such a wonderful feeling. It gives you absolute freedom. You're not beholden to other people's dreams and the desire for more material things.*

Oh, and the girl that caught his eye on his first visit to the garbage dump, Ney Hang, is now a second-year university student and mentors' children at CCF.

Are you ready to become love?

Activity

What, if anything, does the story of Scott Neeson inspire in you? Is there any action you feel called to take to become more loving? Listen to your heart to see if there is a desire to help in any capacity. If there is, act on it. If not, then it will come later. (Everything occurs in its right time.)

Pay attention. As you become love, your heart and mind open and intuitive receptivity gets stronger. There is nothing to interfere with the urgings of Spirit and your sense of guidance is intensified

In the meantime, love all existence without discrimination. Start loving without a reason. Love the trees, the flowers, the earth, everything. Simply radiate love. You become one with the whole Universe and boundaries disappear. See the light in every person. Each one is at his own stage of development and trying his best according to his understanding and experience.

As needs come up in the moment, and there is an urge to respond, do it spontaneously.

Be compassionate.

V - Listening

The choice is yours. You hold the tiller. You can steer the course you choose in the direction of where you want to be— today, tomorrow, or in a distant time to come.

Clement Stone

Dwell on the beauty of life. Watch the stars and see yourself running with them.

Marcus Aurelius, *Meditations*

Summary:

Are you afraid of being alone with yourself? There are people who avoid aloneness like the plague and as a result, they miss out on the benefits that come from creating sacred alone time. Yet being alone with yourself is a primary way to connect with your intuitive channel.

There is power in learning how to be alone and not lonely. Self-acceptance -- really desiring a healthy relationship with self is a necessity to facing your fear of being alone. Learning to be sacred with your alone time helps you focus within. This is where you will discover true bliss.

Do you own stuff, or does it own you? That is the question we ask in this section. To cultivate deep connection, start by eliminating the clutter of egoic fear and useless material stuff. You clear space for positive change by letting go of negativity. That means you must discover the fears that bind in order to cultivate mental impressions that enrich and enliven. The same thing is true of physical space. It must be cleared of useless stuff so the mind can achieve order. To realize highest connection, clear out anything that detracts – tangible or intangible.

More information on intuition is offered including a simple technique to move easily into intuitive perception. Each exercise helps to open and strengthen your intuitive connection.

Often people take life too seriously and view events as tragic, awful, difficult and a big struggle. When you do that you make life all of those things. To move to a place of clarity you must cultivate a sense of lightness. Letting go and lightening your approach becomes a source of happiness, health, and ease of living. Taking a light approach raises your energy and helps you discern truth. You learn how to rise above your situation. Perspective is lost when you become mired in challenges. Yet adjusting your view admits humor. Masters laugh easily and you can too! If there is any doubt, a study is included to make the point.

***

Most people have a terrible time listening. They want to put their meanings and interpretations on everything. It is a form of cognitive dissonance to decide what everything means according to your set ideas while ignoring the facts.

Some avoid inner listening as in meditation. They are afraid of creating a connection to Spirit for fear of what they will discover. Perhaps they are unworthy. In truth, there is nothing to be afraid of because as the listen deeply (open to receive), you realize that you are worthy, and you are loved.

Intuitive listening is a pure form of connecting with highest Consciousness and involves feeling as much as hearing. It is an art and an invaluable skill and can be cultivated. Becoming receptive in this way makes every part of your life better. You start by learning how to be alone.

Aloneness and loneliness are two difference things. There is power in embracing aloneness. Developing skill in this area improves self-acceptance and makes for a healthy personal relationship with self.

Knowing how to be *with* yourself helps you connect to the present moment. Being present and fully centered in yourself elevates your consciousness. The result is bliss.

In this section you are given cues to using your alone time well by listening beyond material conditions (appearances) to your soul essence. In solitude you are able to experience your expanded self. It is a time to self-nurture, heal, and connect deeply. As you do this, your awareness expands beyond physical limits, your ego dissolves, and identification with your small self disappears. Expansiveness is your authentic state.

The idea is to shift your attention to Universal Intelligence where everything is known, and all things are possible. As you build your practice, your ability to remain in an expanded state strengthened and you will feel the connection to Spirit. (It is always present and available.)

The result: your potential to be guided by Highest Intelligence intensifies.

To prepare for this shift, it is imperative to create space. That means to establish the mental/physical conditions to allow change to occur. It means eliminating clutter of every kind. De-cluttering creates space for Deepest Intelligence to speak to you. It is a necessary component to the work you are doing.

Clutter represents chaos. Eliminating it releases confusion, ego fear, demeaning beliefs and useless stuff that take up valuable time and space. De-cluttering frees you.

Clearing mental space allows positive images to immerge. This implies releasing the disorder and craziness of negative beliefs and images. That includes destructive self-talk, gossip, judgments, criticizing – you get the point.

Opening space is part of the process for raising your energy so you can be a conduit for higher consciousness. You must make yourself available, to be open, for high vibrational thoughts to flow through your consciousness. Thus, this step is about opening your channel.

No one functions well in clutter. Whether mental, emotional, or physical, mess and disarray obstruct clarity, creativity, and vision. Tuning in to your deeper knowing mind means making room for love, positivity, and guidance.

The same thing is true of physical space. You need room to organize and think. Dealing with mess in your living area is just as debilitating as having a confused mind. In other words, let go of stuff that is valueless, no longer practical, and has seen its day.

This section will help you to create space for the life you want. Clearing space is a vital and on-going mental-physical practice. It frees you to think and move in flow and to connect more deeply.

As an adjunct to opening space, and just as important, is learning how to just *"be."* It is easy to get caught in the details of life and forget to stop and smell the roses. Yet strengthening the voice of intuition requires removing the masks and various demeanors life requires and learning how to relax into being.

Turning attention inward can only happen by taking time to do so. That means having a plan and setting aside daily time to indulge in quiet so you can listen to stillness (the space between thoughts), find your natural rhythm, and meditate.

Without daily sabbaticals, you become imbalanced - too much doing and not enough being. The result is mental exhaustion, anxiety, and stress. Diligence and self-discipline keep the mind from running amuck in the bowels of despair. It is about balance - rest, quiet, and restoring rhythm and taking time to be.

***

Embrace Aloneness

Are you afraid of being alone? There are people who avoid aloneness like the plague. As a result, they miss out on the benefits that come from experiencing sacred alone time. It is a primary way to cultivate connect with your deepest self.

There is power in learning how to be alone and not lonely. Self-acceptance is derived from developing a healthy relationship with self. It is the key ingredient to facing your fear of being alone. Making your alone time sacred helps you use it well to focus your attention within.

Love resides in your heart and you must be still to find it.

You will discover cues to using your time alone well by learning to listen beyond material appearances. It is a time of luscious nurturing and self-healing. Fear indicates you have not understood the treasure to be found in being alone. For it is through sacred stillness that you find bliss.

The mind is constantly stimulated, busy, and agitated as you focus externally where drama after drama unfolds. We think that being present in the material world with its noise and chaos is the place to be. *I am bored. I need noise, distraction, and stimulation.* The ego cultivates fear of aloneness and demonizes it. *What is wrong with you? You are alone. You must be unloved. You are a loser.*

Lingering in these messages gives you reason to avoid being by yourself. They convince you that being alone is dangerous or wrong. You use it as evidence of being unlovable. You might fear that you are missing out on something if you take time for yourself. You might even fear having a nervous breakdown.

The issue is that we have constructed an identity, a false identity, that is dependent on the superficial world. It started with your name, your gender, and your circumstances. You call yourself an American, an Indian, European, South Sea Islander, or any other cultural signature. You also identify with all sorts of physical attributes, such as tall or short, blonde, grey, or redheaded, as well as with a variety of religious and tribal ethnicities, like Hindu, Jew, Muslim, Sufi, Christian, to name a few. These are superficial distinctions and designed to fool you into believing that these tiny elements are who you are. The whole identity fiasco reigns true until you examine your psyche in a deeper way and gift yourself the adventure of aloneness. To see beyond appearance requires time to contemplate a deeper reality.

The first inclination when you are alone is to call it *loneliness* and you then get busy. You tell yourself, *do something.* Why... because you want to run in fear from loneliness and staying busy is how the ego keeps you distracted. You must be productive, useful, a doer. Do something. Don't just sit there and *be.* Wash windows clean the floor, sort papers, make a phone call. The mind is indoctrinated into busyness and panics when asked to be still. You may even become depressed, telling yourself, *you are without purpose, a bum, lazy, good for nothing. No one will miss you when you are gone.*

These are fear thoughts, conjured up from old programs planted in your subconscious mind. They all relate to some form of identity you have taken on in your past. Now, they rule until you say, *NO.*

Have you ever watched a lion lying on a hill looking out over his domain? He may sit there for hours gazing. He does not feel alone or unproductive because he is tuned in to nature and enjoying his world. He is not lazy because when the time is right, he will spring forward to catch an antelope or mouse. He lets inner intelligence tell him when it is time. You are a lion in your domain. Your power lies in appreciating your power and that can only come through nurturing your spirit.

Thus, the first step in mastering aloneness is to observe and realize the egoic patterns you have been taught that you might address them and be free. As you progress past the fear of being alone, the next step might be to offer yourself to nature.

The natural world is still and rhythmic, primarily peaceful. Go into nature as Jesus went to the mountain or the desert. Go where there is emptiness. That is where you can release the stress of your material life and all that goes with it.

Don't stay for an hour. Linger longer. Stay in the natural world until your mind settles.

Then, stay longer. Remain until your body relaxes and begins to breathe. Then, stay even longer.

Be still. This is where you will have an inner experience that matches the rhythm of nature.

There was a young martial-arts student who was receiving instruction from a famous master. One day, the master observed a practice session and realized the presence of other students seemed to interfere with his student's attempt to perfect his moves. The master sensed the young man's frustration. He went to him, tapped him on the shoulder, and asked, *"What's the problem?"*

The student, obviously stressed, answered, *"I don't know. I keep trying, but I am unable to execute the moves correctly."*

The wise master said to him, *"Before you can master technique, you must understand harmony."* He took the student some distance into the woods where they found a stream. The master stood quietly on the bank for a few minutes before speaking. *"Look at the stream. You see the rocks in its way. Does it smash into them out of frustration? No, the stream merely flows over and around the rocks and moves on. To be in harmony, you must be like the water and you will know what harmony is."*

The young man listened carefully and took the master's advice to heart. Soon, he was barely noticing the other students around him. Nothing could come in the way of focusing in his practice. He executed the most perfect moves.

To be in harmony, as the stream is to the rocks, is our task. It requires stillness. In our Western world, this can be a monumental accomplishment. Not so much in Eastern countries where silence is cultivated. Just grant yourself permission. In time, you will get the hang of it and it will nourish you, even heal you. Stay in the stillness for three days or a week, maybe three months. Remain until you have forgotten all the roles you play and the ways you clothe yourself with identity. Stay until you become nothing, just quiet emptiness.

From this point, you can move into a deeper energy. Let the mind drift into feeling - deep feeling. Feel your breath. Notice its texture, temperature, and rhythm. Feel your body organs function. And feel your spirit. Let it expand so that you are able to move beyond your physical self to feel the space you occupy. Then feel all space. Your mind will begin to change texture as you do this. It becomes softer, lighter. Stay there. No judgment, no anything, just beingness.

Loneliness is not the same as aloneness. Loneliness is always questing after something. It is painful and demoralizing. It is the ego never being enough or having enough. When you cultivate aloneness, you are at peace. It is like dropping all the trappings of the world and listening deeply. There is something that would speak to you. Have you created the inner space for it? Have you opened your heart with wonton desire to receive it? *Be still and know that I am*

God. Be still...be still!

Take time daily to practice aloneness. It will help you put everything into perspective because, when you are alone, nothing else exists. It is like the contentment of being in the womb. Everything is provided. You are safe and nourished. No wonder babies cry when they leave the peace of the womb. They are leaving the Garden of Eden, where there is love and no stress.

As you get stronger, the craziness of the material world will dissolve and what remains will be YOU, vast and still, like the forest at dusk or a clear, calm mountain lake. Be still and you will know yourself. That is the mastery that leads to knowing.

Activity

This activity is simple. Depending on your tolerance, practice being alone. If this is difficult for you, start with an hour or two. Notice your thoughts while you are alone. You can even journal them. Observe what your mind is saying. These are just thought forms, and you don't have to take them for truth, but if you observe what is happening in your mind, you might understand why aloneness could be a problem for you.

If there are negative thoughts, let them flow by without reacting to them. If there are positive thoughts, you can do the same. Be the observer of your thoughts and, with practice, your mind can become neutral. Just practice watching. Soon your mind will be still like a mirrored lake.

As you get better at being alone, notice your breathing and the feelings in your body. Move your attention to your heart and feel its energy. In time, you will be able to experience the presence of a greater energy. Keep practicing. You might even find peace. That is when you will know you have conquered your fear of being alone. You are the master.

***

Clear Space - Inner and Outer

Do you own stuff, or does it own you? That is the question we ask in this chapter. To cultivate inner knowing, start by eliminating the clutter of egoic fear, chatter and useless material stuff. You clear space for positive images by letting go of the clutter of negative ones. That means you must be aware of the fears that bind, so that you can promote mental impressions that enrich and enliven.

The same thing is true of physical space. It must be cleared of junk. (Junk is distracting.) This is about opening up space for a positive life experience. When you are mentally cluttered with worry, anxiety and *"what ifs,"* you will not be able to move to vaster awareness. Clearing space is a necessary mental and physical practice that will free you to develop knowing.

There is a story about a beaver that moved a neighborhood stream. Every day, the beaver took down small trees to add to his dam and his house. He was literally *busy as a beaver* because, in a relatively short time, he accomplished a lot of work. Within a couple of weeks, the small stream had turned into a small pond.

The people in the area thought that, with the beaver's house built, they would see little of him. However, the beaver had other plans. He started chewing on a very large maple tree, one that stood over sixty feet tall and had a diameter of approximately five feet. This beaver had taken on an amazing challenge.

Throughout the winter, he would come out and chew a bit on the tree. There were setbacks with major winter storms and freezing weather, and during those times, he was not seen. The people did not believe he would be able to chew through the giant tree, but relentlessly, the beaver showed up to chew a bit more whenever the sun came out and the weather allowed.

Spring arrived. The neighborhood families gathered to check on the beaver's progress. Sure enough, the tree was going to come down, and soon! The entire tree had been chewed almost completely around and through the trunk.

The beaver had worked, day after day, on what started as a goal of survival: to build a home for the winter. He had clarity of purpose and vision. Yet, when he started chewing on the large maple, he was no longer focused on survival. He was focused on the future. He intended to use the tree for spring, to provide new food and to gather branches to continue damming the stream in preparation for the spring thaw. No matter what obstacles were presented to him, he kept moving toward his goal.

The beaver is a perfect symbol of determination and purpose. Sometimes, like the beaver, our goal is survival, but it eventually transforms into building a new home within ourselves. Along the way, we release the clothes, furniture, habits, and things that no longer represent who we are so that we can adjust our outer expression to reflect our current self.

We let go of old patterns of anger and resentment for the same reason. They interfere with the peace and tolerance of who we want to be. And just like the beaver, we may experience setbacks along the way, but we keep chipping away to shape our internal and external lives.

Pay attention to the dark times when things seem not to work, when your back is up against the wall or plans derail. This is a time of opportunity. Change is in the air. Smell it. Get familiar with it and embrace it. Start the process by letting go of the ego's version of how it should look or be.

The ego, or intellect, is limited in its understanding of possibilities and potentials. Therefore, if you allow it to run your life, you will stay limited and stuck. When things are not moving in the direction you think you want, it is an indication that a new way is opening for you.

You must be ready to take it. There's a new door ready to open and a new path to follow.

This is where *letting go* comes into play. In order to move forward you must let go of the past and that includes all that isn't working. It comprises everything from a dysfunctional belief (everyone *must* like me), to an old way of doing things (putting everyone's needs ahead of your own), to old relationships, (people who bring you down and suck your energy), and to a job you hate and obligations that are joyless. Yes, it is time to clean house, both inside and out.

Your external, material house, when clogged with *stuff*, reflects fear and inadequacy. When you hold on to things that are no longer relevant, you get stuck in an attitude of not being enough. It is a way that you reinforce lack in your life. Your house and your office reflect your state of mind. To create space for new experiences, relationships, and opportunities, you must clean house.

To start the process, designate one room, one drawer, one closet. Set a timer and work for ten minutes. If you are inspired and want to go longer, do it. As you go through the items in the drawer, ask yourself, *"When was the last time I used this. When do I plan to use it again?"* If you haven't used it in the last five years and have no plans on using it in the future, release it.

The key to letting go is to not dwell on the object. If you hold it too long, you could become attached to it. In this exercise, you are working with your *practical* mind. Don't let your emotional, sentimental mind get in the way.

Make assessments and release quickly. Create a stack, box, or bag of items and put them in the trash or recycle them by giving them to friends or an appropriate charity. The clothes that are out of style, no longer fit, and don't reflect who you are, go in this stack. The items in the junk drawer that will never get used, the cookbook that has never been opened, the uncomfortable shoes that will never get worn, all go in this stack. You might feel some sentimental, re-attachment pain. Move through it. The positive result you get from clearing space will pay huge dividends. You will have room to move, plan, or invite someone or something new into your life. You might discover a new club, a workout group, or new friends as your mind opens to greater possibilities.

It has been proven that clutter damages the psyche, and that unhealthiness extends to the body. It is literally and figuratively *moldy*. It symbolizes the moldy past. You cannot be in the present moment with reminders of the past everywhere. Clutter creates pressure because you have to move it or move around it. You often can't find anything amidst the clutter. Does it serve a purpose now? Is there a purpose for it in the new life you are creating?

We also create clutter by holding on to past guilt, shame, and hurt feelings. All of these keep the mind filled with thoughts that are not relevant to the present moment. Forgive and let go. Forgive yourself; forgive others; forgive everyone and everything. It is all a memory, like a stream of air that passes over you. It happened. Now it is gone.

A cluttered environment reflects a cluttered mind. And all clutter is distracting. The reason people become messy or hoard is because they are afraid. They are afraid they are not enough; they will not have enough, and perhaps there will *never* be enough. To move forward, fear must be replaced with love, the opposite of fear. It starts with loving who you are now, in this moment and in this stage of your life. Love your blessings and your daily opportunities to express yourself. Love all that is good in life.

You believe in lack when you say, *"There will never be enough. I am not enough."* This belief, based in fear, is behind clutter.

Our culture is fear-based. All you have to do to prove this is to listen to the news and the way it is presented: lots of drama. It captures your attention if you allow yourself to be a part of it. You've heard the phrase, *If it bleeds, it leads.* Couple that with all the movies and television shows that depict violence, and you have a full spectrum of indoctrination through fear.

Fear has become the dominant energy in this world. It has captured people's thought systems by encouraging the idea of *never enough* and wars that go on forever. It is a kind of sickness that leads to addiction. *But* you can clean house. That means cleaning your mind, your body, and your house.

Why is cleaning and letting go part of self-mastery and knowing, you may ask? To manage and control your mind means handling, by extension, all that is included in your mind: your physical self and your home. If you clutter any of these areas, you are not in full control.

You can start anywhere, but the mind is the likeliest place to begin de-cluttering since a clear mind will help you achieve the clarity required to de-clutter everything else. Start by refusing negative thoughts and judgments. When they show up, shut the door in their face. As former first lady, Nancy Reagan used to instruct, *"Just say NO."*

Opinions go along with negative thoughts. People form their opinions based on beliefs. Some of these are inefficient, useless, and even dishonest. Observe your thoughts and you will discover belief systems that need to go.

For example, you might say, *"I can't handle something or other."* Of course, you can handle whatever you need to.

"It is important that everyone like me." This is a waste of time.

"I can't deal with conflict." You'll be hiding under your bed forever. Get over it.

"What will other people think?" That is not your business.

"What if I do it wrong?" Just do it. You will experience a tremendous freedom.

"I don't want to look foolish." Looking foolish is a figment of your fear-based imagination. The truth is: no one is looking.

Survey your thoughts and beliefs and close the door to those that take up space without offering value.

A new disciple asked his master, *"How do you practice Tao (connecting to God),* Sir?

The master answered, *"When you are hungry, eat. When you are tired, sleep."*

The disciple was incredulous at the simplicity of the answer. *"Isn't that what everyone does?"*

"No," the master replied. *"No. Most people feed themselves with thousands of desires when they eat and dream of thousands of designs when they sleep."*

Manifest plainness, Embrace simplicity.
Put others first.
Desire little.
Lao Tzu, Tao Te Ching

When you find your mind racing from one thing to the next, and your home stuffed with things you will never use, it is your signal to simplify. Simplification means releasing activities and things that do not add to your well-being such as obligatory visits, meetings that take time but don't glean results, events and organizations that are habits but no longer enrich. Most people have too much going on. They are constantly distracted.

Simplify your living environment. What haven't you used in the last year, two years? What have you grown out of that no longer represents your style? This could be clothes, furniture, room arrangements, colors, accessories, art, kitchen utensils, or even your house. It could even be relationships. If you never plan on using your pasta maker, let it go. If you have too much of one thing, like towels or dishes, donate.

Speaking of decisions, don't put them off. Procrastination never turns out well. You want your mind to be clear and not clogged with things to remember or decisions to make. Make decisions quickly. You can always reverse them later, if need be. More than likely, you won't have to.

Do one thing at a time. People tend to think that multi-tasking is a great idea. It isn't. You can best concentrate on one thing at a time. So, do one thing. Then do the next thing. Your focus will be sharper, and you will accomplish your task more efficiently and without error. When you multi-task, you don't really remember what you did because your attention is never really focused.

Now, let's look in the pantry and deal with your diet. It has been proven that inflammation creates disease. Just as your car doesn't run smoothly without the right oil and gasoline, your body doesn't operate efficiently when clogged with sugar and white flour. Get rid of processed foods and all items that do not provide nourishment. You get *foggy-brained* when you contaminate the body with non-nutritious foods. *More greens, please.*

Write things down. There is no need to remember the minutia of life. It clogs your mind trying to remember everyone's phone number and all your appointments. Clear mental space so that you can be open to new creative ideas by writing down the details and keeping an up-to-date calendar and to-do list. Mark through each item that is completed on your list. Your list will never be completed, so, don't worry about it. It is a living, breathing reminder of the things that need to be addressed. If these items are written down, you can deal with them as time allows.

Give yourself time daily to rest. That means no stimulation from the computer or television. Be quiet. Take a walk. Meditate. Let your mind rest.

Set priorities. There are only twenty-four hours in a day. You will not get everything done. Okay! So, decide what the two or three most important items are on your to-do list and concentrate there.

Without setting priorities, you can diddle away a whole day and feel terrible about it.

Clutter is everywhere. It comes in the mail, in emails, in text messages. You might stuff it in drawers and never refer back to it. It may cover your desk. It can choke your efforts to change and stops the flow. Each week pick a drawer, a cupboard, or a pile of papers, and de-clutter it. Soon you will have created a habit of letting go and your mind will be clear. Letting go of clutter is the same as letting go of fear. To be a master and manage your mind, you must be selective with your thoughts. It makes sense to be selective with everything else as well.

I knew a woman I shall call Peggy. She was a full-blown hoarder. Her daughter reported that, to get through her house, you had to follow a narrow path that wound through magazines, boxes, and all sorts of rubble. About once a month, the plumbing in the bathroom would get clogged with tree roots and the Roto-Rooter man would come out to snake the plumbing lines and open them up again.

The cluttered house represented a metaphor for Peggy. She housed remorse and shame, as well as lots of fears, which clogged her mental, emotional, and physical being. When I asked her about her clutter, she informed me that, *"If anyone comes into my house to harm me, they will never find me."*

Another time, she told me that carrying extra weight on her body made her unattractive so that no one would approach her. In other words, she was premeditated in making sure that no one would be drawn to her. You get the idea that Peggy carried a lot of fear.

One day, Peggy had a heart attack. When the doctors viewed the results of her tests, they found she had major heart blockages and needed a triple-heart bypass to survive. Even her heart was cluttered. Peggy had the surgery and recovered. Hence, her immediate health challenge was handled. But that was just for the moment.

Interestingly enough, Peggy understood that her fear, which was reflected in hoarding, was behind her physical problems, but she was still unable or unwilling to let go and make changes in her life.

My assessment of Peggy was she has always believed herself to be wrong, the guilty party, no matter what. Overwhelmed with guilt and shame, she used clutter to hide.

When it comes to mastering the mind and moving into our deepest consciousness, it is important to note that fear is *concocted*, a mental construct, imagined. For the most part, fear is *False Evidence Appearing Real,* and it incapacitates the person housing it. Most fears are completely useless and will never happen. It is highly doubtful that anyone will enter Peggy's home to do her harm. Just like no one will drag her out of hiding. By entertaining these imagined fears, she lowers the quality and vibrancy of her life. She becomes dysfunctional and unhealthy.

And she even protects her dysfunction by pretending to hide it mounds of rubble.

On the other hand, there are legitimate fears, like having to drive on icy roads. In that case, you develop a reasonable strategy to deal with it. You slow down, take safe routes, or stay home. You don't visualize crashing into vehicles and flipping over on the side of the road. You don't direct your mind to linger on what you don't want to happen. Instead, you handle the challenge as it appears. Wouldn't it be ridiculous to be afraid of icy roads when you are experiencing sun-shiny days 90-degree temperatures in July?

When I realized that I had a fear of the dark, I traced it back to the idea of *The Boogie Man.* My mother had invented this imaginary fellow when I was a child to make sure my siblings and I didn't leave the house after dark. Interestingly enough, there are many ways parents use fear to *keep their kids safe*. It is a dichotomy and often works in reverse – in creating more fear.

When I discovered the Boogie Man in my psyche, I decided that, first, he did not exist, and second, I was going to aggressively challenge my fear of the dark. Even though I knew the Boogie Man was made up, the fear of him (or danger) had been well planted in my mind for a long time. I was going to have to face this fear repeatedly to be done with it and I was okay with that.

In that regard, I made a practice of walking into the dark house when I came home at night. I would give myself several minutes to be in the dark and notice that nothing bad happened before I flicked on the light. I took it further and ventured into the dark and noticed my feelings. I stayed there until the fear dissolved. After a month or two, I was no longer afraid of the dark because I willingly explored it and discovered no threat. In challenging fear, I built a new brain pathway that accepted darkness as safe and comforting.

A friend of mine, who happened to be an Army Ranger, showed me that when I got used to being outside in the dark, my eyes acclimated to the light of the moon and stars and I could see pretty well. So, all in all, I am fine in the dark. But you can see by this story that, if you want to let go of fear that has been around for a long time, you must face it repeatedly until you have constructed a new understanding.

Releasing clutter on all levels – physically, mentally, emotionally – will give you the command you need to develop mind mastery. That is required to easily move into deeper levels– highest consciousness, intuition.

Activity

1. Discover your fear. Is it darkness, or confrontation, or being alone? Devise a plan to challenge it.

With the darkness, you could follow my tactic of familiarizing yourself with it. With confrontation, you may have to start asking for what you want. You can do this by using "I" statements. No one is threatened when you state your desire using the word "I."

> *"I could use some help."*
> *"When you do that, I feel uncomfortable."*
> *"I feel sad that we are having trouble talking or working together."*

Start with a benign situation for practice and become bolder as you get stronger. At the grocery store or bookstore, you might speak up and say, *"Excuse me, I think you gave me the wrong change."*

If you are afraid of being alone, spend time alone. Start small with fifteen or thirty minutes. Notice what seems scary about it. Stay with the fear until it dissolves. As you breathe and focus in the present moment, fear dissolves.

By facing fear, you are de-cluttering mentally and emotionally. This de-cluttering process makes room for positive energy and thoughts. You release fear; you make room for love!

2. Start de-cluttering something in your life by picking a drawer, cabinet, closet, or stack of paper. Set a timer to go through it. Let go of everything that hasn't been used in the last five years and won't be used in the next 12 months. Move quickly so you don't reattach to anything and start the memory chain. Be of generous spirit. If you are not going to use it, perhaps it will work for someone else.

As with all transformational exercises, keep a journal and write notes on how things unfold. What was your reaction? How did you deal with it? What is your next step?

***

More Insight on Intuition

There is an interesting fact regarding energy. As you look out at the world, energy is continually flashing back and forth between your eyes. If you were to focus on one item only and hold your attention on it for at least thirty seconds, this flashing energy would settle and transfer to the pituitary gland just behind the eyes. The pituitary gland is the center for "inner sight." Quieting your eyes is an easy way to direct energy to the pituitary gland, third eye, or intuitive eye. Focusing energy to the pituitary immediately links you to your intuitive faculty.

Yes, by holding your eyes motionless for a minimum of thirty seconds, the erratic energy stills and activates intuitive sight. This is why creative people will gaze out the window, appearing to be doing nothing, but they are connecting to higher insight. Or they might ride out to the quiet countryside, or stare at their project, not even registering someone speaking to them. They become transfixed, as in a trance, and creative ideas flow to them. Creativity flows from the inner intuitive faculty to the outer conscious mind. It is how art, music, and all creative endeavors are born. Everything starts with an idea.

The more you engage your intuition, the stronger it becomes. In so doing, you are developing the ability to *know* beyond the present moment, and you are channeling the deep, fine energy of inspiration. Intuition is the voice of God. Conscious, focused connection with this inner voice is the path to freedom and peace.

Writer, actor, director Quentin Tarantino, credits intuition with saving his mother's life.

Tarantino regularly called his mother in the evening to check in and make sure she was all right. But one day, he had a strong sensation to call her at that moment, which he did. His mom answered the phone and she was experiencing pain. As it turned out, she was having a heart attack. Tarantino quickly got help and his mom survived the event.

Quentin Tarantino always pays attention to the still, small voice of intuition. Because he listened, he not only saved his mother's life but manifested many creative ideas which he ultimately produced into movies.

Angela Artemis demonstrates another example of using intuition. She had been offered a well-paying job. After she had accepted the job, she became deathly ill. She couldn't get out of bed for a week. During that time, she experienced tremendous anxiety about taking the job and started to rethink the whole proposition. She knew that everything happened for a reason and, even though the well-paying managerial position seemed perfect, something kept her from moving forward with it. She decided to decline the job.

As it turned out, the company hiring her was in the midst of a merger with another company, and this merger was supposed to make Angela's position lucrative. But something did not seem right. Months after everything was to be signed and completed, it appeared that the merger was on hold and the people who were hired in anticipation of having a spectacular year, were not having a great year at all. They were stuck on the sidelines, waiting for this merger to take place and losing the income that was promised.

In retrospect, Angela's intuition knew best. By following it, she saved herself upset, disappointment, and money - all because she *listened*.

Kara Thompson also followed her intuition to increase her mediumship services. Kara had been asking for guidance on how to expand her business when the name of an acquaintance popped into her mind. This person ran a metaphysical store in Kara's town and was a gifted intuitive. She had done readings for Kara in the past, but they had never done business together.

Consequently, even though she was nervous, Kara followed her guidance and called the woman.

As it turned out, the storeowner was delighted to hear from Kara. She was working on her fall workshop schedule when she received the call. Without even checking the course outline, she happily offered Kara's "Contacting Spirit Guides" class to her store clients.

Emboldened by the owner's enthusiasm, Kara asked if she might be interested in Kara giving group mediumship readings.

Again, the owner was delighted to include Kara's offering and even encouraged her to reach out to larger groups. Hence, by following her inner voice and making one phone call, Kara's services were dynamically expanded.

Do these stories remind you of times when you were guided intuitively? Did you pay attention? What happened? Are you ready to engage your intuition now?

I have used intuition in my work as a counselor, coach, Akashic Record Reader, and educator for over 40 years. I think of it as tuning my mind as you would a radio. If you want a specific radio station, you set your dial to that station. The radio is an instrument that follows your instruction and picks up the specific frequency you set the dial on.

The mind does the same thing. If you have developed control of your attention, you are able to tune to a particular human frequency and read the energy of that person or event. This "read-out" can present in words, pictures, feelings, or all of the above. The key to accuracy is keeping your opinionated egoic, intellectual mind out of the way. To access the pure flow of intuition takes practice and it also keeps your attention above the fray of where most people spend their time – in fear, chaos, and confusion.

Deep inner connection can help you know what to do and when to do it. It helps you transform beliefs and release confusion. It connects you to the causes of events and circumstances so that you can adjust your thinking, and emotional status to bring about dynamic change. It deepens your relationship to Spirit and helps you release negativity, guilt, and dysfunctional, disempowering thoughts. It gives you the higher view of what is really happening and what are the possibilities. It is enlightening and evolutionary.

Activity

This exercise will help you strengthen your concentration and focus your mind. Gaze at something—a flower, a gem, the sky, or candle flame—and hold your attention on it for thirty seconds or more. If you get distracted wait for your eyes to become quiet. Then continue focusing on the object or sky. As your eyes become still, the energy automatically moves to the pituitary gland, the center of inner sight. Thus, you have triggered intuition, the link to your Higher Mind.

Lengthen the time you sit and gaze daily. Notice the space into which you mentally shift. It is quiet and calming. Get familiar with it. You will find it relaxing and inspiring. Soon, as you gaze, you will find a new door has opened. It is the space of inner knowing.

Stay with this exercise for a while and it will lead you into a deep form of meditation. In time, as you focus, you may feel the desire to close your eyes. When this happens, continue to stay focused on the peaceful space you have discovered.

A variation on this exercise can be used after you have trained your attention for a month or so. Think of a subject you would like to understand in greater depth. This can also be a question. Once you have received your answer or information, let go and continue to focus in this inner space. You are strengthening your intuitive channel. You will find it to be a great resource as you move through life.

Be patient and allow your intuitive channel to develop. There is no strain to this. If you are straining, you are thinking. Intuition requires space. When you have made the connection, the answers will flow. Just stay open.

***

The Body as an Antenna

The body is like an antenna. It is ever connected to your inner intelligence (knowing) and the quantum field of energy in which you live. In fact, the body's main function is communication. It is always relaying information to be noted and processed.

We have all seen animals who sense when their owners are returning home and run to the door or window to greet them. They also know ahead of time when the delivery or mail person is approaching. They don't know this because they have thought about it. They know it because they sense it. They are tuned in to this vast field of knowledge and awareness in which we live and have no qualms in accepting it. They KNOW what is going on at all times.

We are just like these animals. In fact, we are part animal (the body and instinctive thinking represent our animal nature). By listening to your body's intelligence, you can tune-in to your current state of being and health.

Illness is not random. It doesn't attack you or show up for no reason. It is the result of various factors. Some are environmental and others purely mental/emotional. For instance, if you hate your job and you find your boss oppressive, yet every day you go to work feeling trapped and squashed, your body will unerringly play out this accumulated stress and repression. It reveals this oppression through organic wear and tear and/or illness. Headaches, body aches, low immunity, inability to sleep are all patterns of stress.

Have you ever heard someone say, *I'm sick of this!* Well! That is exactly what is happening. In other words, there is a price to pay for living or working in unpleasant, harsh conditions, and the body is showing you the price.

The point here is to listen to the body's intelligence. It is another way to note beyond reasoning or intellectuality what is going on. The body will also tell you when someone is lying. You will notice a *"bad"* feeling, like an emptiness, when a person fudges on the truth. It may also feel like clutching, resistance, or a knot in your stomach.

Often, we rationalize these feeling, but the better way is to pay attention and connect them to what is going on. We have all met people that immediately exuded creepiness. We may not even know what the creepiness is, and you don't need to. Just pay attention and keep yourself safe. NEVER go against these feelings. NEVER!!! Just note that if there is a "creepy" feeling, there is a reason for it, and stay clear. It doesn't matter how charming or charismatic the person in question is, pay attention to the creepy feeling.

The same thing is true if you are invited to a party or a meeting and you get a bad feeling. Ask your inner intelligence, what is this about, and as you cultivate deeper listening, you will know the answer.

Activity

Make it a practice to check in with your body several times throughout the day. When you are given a project, check your feelings. Feeling anxiety about performing is not the same as feeling creepy. When you meet a new person, what do you feel? Most people are well-intentioned, and you will feel fine. Checking your feelings is a simple thing to do and will let you quickly know that you are on track, or not.

***

Cultivate Lightness of Being

Often people take life too seriously and view events as tragic, awful, difficult and a struggle. If and when you do that you make life all of those things. To move to a place of simplicity and clarity you must cultivate lightness of being. It is a source of happiness, health, and ease of living. It is also the way you release mental clutter and access higher intelligence/intuition.

Taking a light approach raises your energy and helps you discern truth. It helps you rise above your situation, relax, and tune-in to subtler energy. You lose perspective when mired in ideas that life I a struggle and has to be hard. How can you adjust your view to find humor?

Enlightened masters laugh easily, and you can too!

There are many principles offered in this book, along with activities to incorporate them into your life. These ideologies are the result of a lifetime of research, discovery, and practice. By integrating them into your practice, you give yourself the greatest gift you could ever hope to have – a deep intuitive connection to Spirit. This connection will take you to new heights of awareness and expansion, love, joy and peace. It will shift your life from worry and angst to the high energy of bliss.

You are in a growth process. It is my desire that you be patient as you develop each activity and approach. You are reshaping, reprogramming, and re-setting your mind and that takes time and practice.

In the process, you are constructing a new you. This new you is free from ego constraints of judgment, and angst over things that cannot be changed and are ultimately irrelevant. As you transform, your light radiates brighter. That is a gift to you and to the world.

Understanding the laws of the universe is imperative to living a joy-filled life. As you experiment with universal law, you discover what works and what doesn't. You begin to know when to step forward and when to let go and let God. All things are possible through God. So, you include highest intelligence / God in every endeavor. That is true partnership and power.

In this section, we are focusing on light-heartedness, laughter, hugs, and seeing with new eyes. The lighter you are, the easier it is to access higher intelligence. It does not come to a mind clamped down with fear and worry. Enlightened masters know how to laugh at life and themselves. We must do the same.

There are many ways to cope with everyday pressures. One of the more fun methods is laughing. In his book, *Anatomy of An Illness,* Norman Cousins made the point that laughter is good medicine. When faced with a terminal illness, Cousins healed himself by watching humorous movies.

The idea of raising his energy through laughter turned out to be an effective healing technique. It worked. Since then, others have picked up on the concept and taken additional steps to assist folks integrate laughter as a stress reliever.

In Columbus, Ohio, psychologist Dr. Steven Wilson and a group of health professionals formed the *World Laughter Tour* to assist people in improving their physical and mental health through systematic laughter. As part of this movement, there are Laughter Clubs forming and even Laugh Yoga.

It appears that mental and physical wellness requires joviality, and the more we laugh, the happier we become. Many comedians speak of having tough times as children, living in poverty, and struggling to have enough food. Their comic performances began by learning to look at the ridiculous side of things, and they basically laughed their way out of scarcity. They actually opened their minds to a larger view when they did this.

Rodney Dangerfield is a prime example. His father, a comedian and juggler, left the family shortly after Rodney's birth, leaving his mother to raise their children alone. To help the family scrape by, Rodney began selling ice cream on the beach and delivering groceries after school. He struggled through a difficult childhood and was often the focus of torment from anti-Semitic teachers and more affluent students.

To cope, he began writing jokes, illustrating the point that humor really can save us. At seventeen, he started performing his act on amateur nights in various clubs. By the age of twenty-nine, Rodney was performing a full-time act under the stage name Jack Roy. Comedy, however, did not pay well and when he married and had two children, he quit to become an aluminum-siding salesperson. I am sure he produced a lot of comedic patter from being in sales.

Even though he had struggled, Rodney continued to feel drawn to comedy and eventually rehabilitated his career. He worked as a salesman by day and did stand-up comedy at night. That is when the pseudonym, Rodney Dangerfield, was created. The name referenced a joke by comedian Jack Benny.

Dangerfield trusted his inner drive (intuition/creativity) and finally got his big break in the early 1970's, when *The Ed Sullivan Show* tapped him to perform. 4433He was an immediate hit with audiences, and his *No-Respect* statement became his tag line going forward.

Many comedians had similar trials growing up, and they turned to comedy to bring laughter to their seemingly dark worlds. They helped the world laugh while they used humor as their own way out. They proved that lightness of being helps and heals. When they laughed, they felt better. We all feel better when we laugh.

There is scientific evidence that the body benefits from lightness of spirit. Dr. Lee Berk in the College of Medicine at the University of California, Irvine, says there are many benefits to laughter. *Your heart rate elevates, blood pressure increases, muscles contract, and oxygen levels rise.* Regular laughter can change the area of the brain that releases stress hormones, and a person becomes better conditioned to handle stress.

For most people, somewhere between childhood and adulthood they forget their joyful side while concurrently tuning out their creative-intuitive voice. The average child laughs or smiles 400 times a day. The average adult laughs fifteen times a day. In the midst of growing up, something gets lost, and many aren't sure how to reclaim it.

Here are some suggestions for bringing lightness into your life:

- Force yourself to laugh. Look into the mirror and vow to make that person laugh, particularly at yourself. It builds humility and humor. Even forced laughter brings health benefits.
- Learn to relax. Stop several times each day to take deep breaths. Affirm, *"I am calm and relaxed."* Repeat these words several times. Within sixty seconds, you will feel better.
- Remember funny moments. Install whimsy in your so you will be reminded to lighten up.
- Watch funny movies and videos (cat videos on YouTube?!)
- Choose to be around light-hearted people.
- Encourage laughter in others. When they laugh, you laugh. (Learn a joke and share it.)

Giving and receiving affection also helps you lighten up. Perhaps you were not raised in an affectionate family (I wasn't) and the idea of hugging people may seem foreign. If so, it might be time to reconsider the value of a hug. (As Meagan Markle puts it, American hug!) Here is a story that makes this point perfectly.

A set of premature twins were parted after birth and placed in separate incubators. One twin was not doing well and wasn't expected to live. Fortunately, a nurse in the preemie nursery decided to break the hospital rules and reunited the two babies. She placed them together in one incubator.

Once they were placed together, the healthier baby threw her arm around her sister. It seemed to be a simple, heartwarming embrace but drew immediate results. The smaller, weaker twin's heart rate grew stronger and stabilized, and her temperature rose to normal. You might conclude that affection and connection saved the weak baby. These are the documented instances that illustrate the necessity, and power, of bringing lightness and laughter into your life.

We've often heard, and possibly suspected, that babies need to be cuddled in order to survive. What we may not have considered is that all people require warmth, nurturing, and compassion. These are the qualities that transfer through a hug, affection, a smile, and a joke. In other words, taking yourself too seriously can be detrimental to your mental-emotional-physical health.

To prove these results, try your own experiment. On a daily basis, give smiles, complements, affirmation and/or hugs. You can set a beginning goal of giving warmth, openness, and/or humor to at least five people a day. Every day offer heartfelt energy to everyone you encounter. Observe your own health and mood as you go along. If you feel lighter and happier, make note. Notice also if you are affecting others. Like one baby hugging another, you may decide to bring your light into the world as you explore this process of giving it away to others. In this way the whole world lightens

Comedian Andy Dooley went so far as to make a *"Free Hugs Here"* sign and hung out at Disneyworld where he gave out hundreds of hugs and had a ball.

If you study spiritual masters and enlightened beings, you will note that they exude lightness, playfulness, and joy. These are important qualities to nurture because they keep you in an open, childlike state of innocence.

Recently I viewed a photo of The Dalai Lama teasing Bishop Desmond Tutu. While posing for photos, he would tease Tutu by lifting his hat from his head and they laughed playfully like little children. Can you remember ever seeing either of them without a smile? They always appear to have a twinkle in their eyes and a smile on their faces. Each has gone through tremendous, life altering struggles and yet their wise, playful essence comes through in every instance. You can do this too and it is important if you want to access the lighter, exalted energy of intuition.

Our original and natural state as babies is joy. With a bit of effort, we can revert back to joy. As babies we were also naturally tuned-in to intuitive intelligence. It guided us on how to roll over, stand up in our crib, mimic language, etc.

Life is basically simple. When we stay in the moment, enjoying beauty, silliness, flow, and tenderness, we feel the connectedness of Spirit.

As you take yourself and the world lightly, your circumstances improve and your options for happiness increase. Lightening your mental load (giving up anger, frustration, and fear) opens you to greater awareness – solutions, answers, creativity.

The happiest people don't necessarily have the best of everything. They *make* the best of everything.

Activity
1. Pick out an area of challenge in your life, perhaps a bill that needs to be paid or a task that must be completed. Look at this challenge from different perspectives.

   How would a child see it? A child might consider a grownup that works at a job his whole life so he can retire, a bit crazy. How would a great leader perceive it? How would someone who grew up in a mud hut and scrapped for food everyday see it? How would God see it?
   Explore different perspectives until you find a way to let go of heaviness. You might even consider the upside of the situation as in" What is the blessing?"
   Indicate here the challenge you will view from different perspectives:

1. Make a point to be around light-hearted people. Or, find something funny to laugh at on television. (*No! Not the news.*) You might read a funny book or conjure a funny angle to something that happened today and share it.

2. Smile, affirm, or hug at least five people every day.

VI. Qualities of a Master

Whatever your mind can conceive and believe, you can achieve.
Napoleon Hill

The mind is a tool. The question is, do you use the tool or does the tool you use.
Zen proverb

Summary:

Why is it important to understand the qualities of a master? Simply because that is where you are headed. The more you sharpen your intuitive faculty, become objective with life, let go of the small stuff so that you can concentrate on what really matters, the closer you come to mastership. What are you mastering – yourself! Why do you want this – because that is how you create the life you want and move into the high energy of Spirit. It is the place of clarity, peace, joy, abundance, wisdom, and confidence. It is what you have always sought and deeply desired.

As you explore the qualities of a master, you will find you possess some of these and may choose to hone even more. You are destined for mastership. Learning to let go of negative judgments, resistance to life, and attachment to temporal things, will free and condition your mind. Learning to forgive is easier than you think and brings ease and harmony. You really can live in peace, connected to higher mind and without the continuous chatter of the ego. These are the practices that will take you there.

***

From the time of creation, you have had the ability to use channel your highest intelligence. It has always been within you and available, but it is of no use, purpose, or benefit until you become consciously aware of its presence. It is as if you have inherited a fortune, but no one informed you of it and, thus, it has not served you in any way. As you open your mind, you will discover the treasure of your intuitive awareness. You will be able to cultivate and strengthen it, and it will serve you like the greatest treasure possible. You will know beyond knowing. You will connect to who you really are – a master.

Why is it important to understand the qualities of a master? Simply, because that is where you are headed. The more you sharpen your intuitive faculty, become objective with life, let go of the small stuff so that you can concentrate on what really matters, the closer you come to mastership.

What are you mastering – yourself! Why do you want this – because that is how you create the life you desire and merge into the high energy of Spirit. It is the place of clarity, peace, joy, abundance, wisdom, and confidence. It is what you have always sought and deeply desired. As you explore the qualities of a master, you will find you possess some of these and may choose to hone more of them. You are destined for mastership. Connection to your Higher

Self is the path, mastership the destination.

Let Go of Judgment

Holding negative judgments and criticism keeps you trapped in your analytical mind. That means connecting with your inner brilliance and creativity is out of the question. Using the suggestions given in this section, will assist you to clear out negativity and the fear it is rooted in, and open to the deeper truth of intuition.

Judgmental people are miserable. Their need to judge is based in personal insecurity and keeps them small and insignificant. It is a sign of fear-based thinking. *I must be right, so you have to be wrong.* Sorry - you can't become strong and secure by focusing on others' flaws. It is the ultimate waste of time.

You have the capacity to live a joy-filled life. Holding to negative judgments clutters your mind with toxic energy, blocks your way, and limits the experience of miracles in your life. Learning to become non-judgmental, seeing neither good nor bad, accepting what is, builds the power of discernment. You literally walk from the miserable prison of judgment to become mentally free. I present this concept because it is an important step to clearing inner space and developing receptivity to Higher Consciousness.

A great teacher once admonished, *Judge not, lest you be judged.* The edict implies that we are better off not judging anyone, including ourselves. Most of the time, we have little evidence to support our judgments. That puts us behind the eight ball in that our judgments always come back to bite us. They also create negative energy in our lives.

Here is a story from the internet. Whether or not it is true, I'm sharing it with you because it makes a great point.

In a grocery store, there was a long line at the cashier counter. An older man near the back sniffed indignantly, *"Some people are so pathetic."*

A young lady at the front of the checkout line repeatedly swiped her credit card. Each time, the machine rejected it. She appeared panicked but continued swiping her card.

"Humph," the older man said with annoyance, making no attempt to conceal his disgust, *"it is one of those welfare people. She should get a job like everyone else."*

The young woman, clearly upset, looked up at the grimacing man. Her eyes welled with tears.

The contemptuous man brazenly stepped forward and announced, *"It was me. I said it."*

With that, the young lady dropped her groceries and her welfare card and ran from the store.

Another person observed the incident with a completely different reaction. He had discovered long ago to never judge anyone, since rarely did he have all the facts. In other words, the tendency is to misjudge when we don't know the details.

A few minutes later, a young man hurried into the store and stopped to describe the young lady to the cashier. *"Have you seen her?"* he asked.

"She ran from the store, got into her car, and sped away."

Scratching his chin, he queried, *"Why would she do that?"*

Everyone turned to the older man who had made the rude remarks. He sheepishly admitted, *"I made a stupid comment about the welfare card she was using. I shouldn't have done it."*

The younger man seemed deeply concerned. *"That is really upsetting. That young woman's brother was killed in Iraq two years ago, and she took on the responsibility of raising his children. She is only twenty years old, single, and struggling, trying to support them all. She doesn't need any more stress."*

The arrogance immediately dissolved in the older man. *"I am so sorry. I was foolish and thoughtless. I didn't realize..."* His tough demeanor melted into shame and guilt.

The young man spoke to the clerk, *"Are these her groceries? Are they paid for?"*

"No," she said a bit rattled, *"the machine wouldn't take her card."*

He reached into his pocket and pulled out a credit card. *"Here take this. I want to pay for her groceries."*

The gentleman who had made the crass remarks stepped forward. *"Do you know her? Do you know where she lives?"*

"Yes, she is my neighbor."

"Wait," the gentleman said. He stepped up to the cashier with his own credit card in hand. *"Please, allow me to pay for these groceries. And, also, please include these on the bill. He began placing his own groceries on the conveyor belt."*

The people in line started putting more groceries on the belt, and others began bagging them.

A woman called out, *"I will get more milk."*

The older man shouted, *"No!"*

Everyone froze.

He called out, *"Get a turkey and a ham, too."*

Everyone started laughing, for now they had joined in a common purpose.

At the end, the bill was over $900. But before the young man could leave with the purchases, the older gentleman stopped him and handed him a check for $1000. *"She is going to need a freezer for all this food."*

The young man looked shocked. *"This is very generous of you,"* he said.

"No," the man answered, *"she is the generous one, and so was her brother."*

With that, everyone broke out in applause. That day, a great lesson was learned about judgment and generosity.

These are important lessons and often not easily understood. Setting aside preconceived notions and uninformed conclusions is a great way to start practicing non-judgment.

Many people habitually get wadded up in judgments. Often, they do this with little information. And unfortunately, most of their judgments weigh on the negative. It creates mental toxicity and a life of drama.

I see this often in relationships. One person judges the other without checking facts. It all relates to whatever injustice he believes he has experienced at the hands of his partner. Most of it is mental fabrication. In other words, whatever one person is doing goes against the ethics, morals, values, expectations, or rules of the other. The judger keeps himself upset because of his stilted interpretation of the actions of another, over which he has no control. He/she makes the other person wrong, so he/she can stand tall in his/her rightness.

"He is selfish – possessive – controlling..."

"She hurt me when she did this or said that, and that means blah, blah, blah."

Rarely, are these conclusions checked to ascertain accuracy. In almost all cases, reactionary statements are made out of pain and a cry for love. Think of the gruff older man who wanted to get through the grocery line quickly and jumped to hurtful conclusions.

There is an art to communication. Stop reacting and ask, *"What is this person saying about himself?"* Most people consider every statement everyone makes as being about *him*. This, of course, makes him the center of everyone else's world. Not likely. More likely, every statement is about the speaker and an attempt to be understood. Understanding this basic premise regarding communication can take the sting out of what might appear as an attack.

Through judgments, people attempt to control events to the point that many of life's gifts are overlooked. When the older man said, *"Some people are so pathetic,"* it was his attempt to move the grocery line forward and, like so many snide remarks, it was ineffective and inappropriate. So, preoccupied with what everyone else *should* be doing, folks ignore their own actions and miss their lessons. Yet, every event and circumstance is rife with opportunities to learn, prosper, and expand in some way.

Perhaps, if each one makes a commitment to put off judgment and replace it with openness, he could get off his emotional roller coaster and experience the natural rhythm and peaceful flow of life. In that way, the incredible bountiful blessings life offers would become more obvious. In the previous story, the blessing was to help another person and to feel good in the process.

Here is another story. See what point it is making. It is a Buddhist story about a pair of acrobats. The teacher was a poor widower and the student was a young lady named Mela. To make money, these acrobats performed daily on the streets.

One of their tricks entailed the teacher balancing a tall bamboo pole on his head while Mela climbed slowly to the top. Once she was positioned on top of the pole, she remained there as the teacher walked forward. To successfully complete the act without injury, both performers had to maintain strong focus and balance.

One day, the teacher said to the young girl, *"I will watch you and you watch me, so that we can help each other sustain concentration and balance. That way, we will make enough money to eat."*

But the student was wise. She answered, *"Dear master, I think it would be better for us to watch ourselves. To look after oneself means to look after both of us. That way, we will avoid any accident and earn enough to eat."*

This story illustrates that taking care of yourself is the best way to take care of others. As you nurture your mind and body, you naturally treat those around you with more compassion and kindness. That is how you will create a positive impact on the world. This self-care includes mindfulness, whereby you take care of your own business and allow others to do the same…without judgment.

Judgment in itself isn't bad. For instance, we have to make a judgment to decide what class to take, what work to engage in, or who to hang out with. Yet, judgment turns negative when you choose to use it to make others bad or wrong or to make yourself right and perfect. Ask yourself if your judgments are helpful or hurtful? What are the intentions behind your judgments?

Holy books suggest that we, *Judge not, lest we be judged.* That means that we are living with our judgments. In other words, whatever you see in others is also in you. As you judge them, you are also judging yourself. If you dislike something about another, you also possess the same quality. Indeed, others are mirrors, reflecting back the things you find appealing or disturbing about yourself.

Lisa became irate when her husband, Joseph, criticized her. Whenever he stormed into the house and complained about the messy rooms or why toys were everywhere, she flinched and became angry.

As she and I conversed, it was clear that Lisa was more critical of herself than she was of her husband. Yet, she was also critical of him. Neither Lisa nor Joseph accepted their own position. Lisa wanted to be out and about, creating a business and feeling inspired. She felt trapped by the traditional view of her role as wife and mother. Once she realized she had choices in how she wanted to manage her responsibilities, she was able to create a new vision for her life.

Joseph resented his job and the amount of travel away from his family it required. Both were unhappy and blamed each other. Both looked outside of self for the cause and could not find it because it was personal and internal. Neither was being honest.

Lisa was the one who broke through and decided to live the life she wanted. She put *creating financial, emotional, and spiritual freedom* at the top of her priority list. As she embraced her ability to make this choice, she no longer responded to Joseph's anger and criticism.

Joseph, on his part, had to decide if he wanted to continue blaming Lisa for his unhappiness or look at himself. The jury is still out on that one. But the fact that Lisa is formulating her own path will ultimately put the ball in Joseph's court. His life will not get better until he faces himself and becomes a kinder person and honest with himself.

A *Course in Miracles* instructs us that judging others is a form of attack. We attack with our thoughts. The term is *attack thoughts*. We certainly cannot consider negative judgments as love.

The opposite of love is fear. Therefore, negative judgments that presuppose others wrong or bad are an expression of fear and a form of attack. We make others bad so we can be right or good. It is a way to bolster the ego. It never feels good. Consequently, to love unconditionally, both yourself and others, don't judge. There is a Native American Indian saying that suggests walking a mile in the other's moccasins before you cast judgment. That idea could waylay judgment, for sure.

In order to live in Highest Consciousness, we will have to desist in making harsh, critical judgments as negative energy poses a barrier to living in joy. Let's consider what you would need to do to love the other person and yourself, to see goodness in them and you.

Make it a practice to find positive qualities in all people you meet. Surely, they love their mothers, parents, or children. Are they polite to strangers? Do they care for their pet?

If you note a behavior about another person, such as being late, that is not a judgment. It becomes a judgment when you decide the person is unworthy or bad because he is late. An observation is different from a judgment. Observations have no toxic energy; judgments do.

Endeavor to seek higher understanding and compassion. You are not in the earth to change others. You are here to learn to love profoundly and, thereby, live a joyful life.

Would you like to discover what your judgments are? Look at the topics below to determine your judgmental triggers. Are you willing to release judgment and replace it with compassion and open heartedness?

Write down your judgment concerning each topic:
- People who are late…
- Being overweight…
- Nosy neighbors…
- Having money to pay the bills…
- Discovering a big stain on your favorite outfit…
- Smoking…
- Wealthy people…
- Conflict…
- Illness…
- The government…
- Critical people…
- The national debt…
- Unwed mothers…
- Welfare…
- Being out of control emotionally…
- Divorce…
- Homosexuality…
- Abortion…
- Bankruptcy…

Can you find the root of fear behind negative judgments? If so, of what are you afraid?

Looking at the examples (stories) offered in this section can you spot the shift each person made to let go of fear and manage his own business? Can you draw any conclusions for yourself from these stories? What can you do to shift your focus from fear to love?

Activity

When you find yourself judging others or being hard on yourself, stop, take a breath, and move into the stillness within.

Go to your heart and feel the love that is there. Send love energy to the person with whom you feel disharmony, even if it is you. Say to yourself, *I bless you and I forgive you for anything real or imagined you have done. I now relax into the Love of the universe and let go.* Feel yourself letting go, like a clenched fist that is opening. Repeat this activity until you have fully let go.

Take note of one of the areas above that you find yourself in negative judgment. Make a conscious decision to let go of judgment on that topic. Then, choose another subject and release judgment on that. Keep releasing judgment until your mind is free and open, and you can observe the world as a beautiful place.

The more you do these exercises, the easier giving up judgment becomes. Peace is far more comforting and enjoyable than discord. Where you place your mind is what you choose to experience.

***

Non-Attachment Frees You

Non-attachment is a high spiritual principle that allows God to work in your life. It is your key to becoming a co-creator with the universe. Letting go of opinions, erroneous beliefs, commitments to obligations that don't enrich, and material objects that bog you down, frees the soul and the mind and creates space for the natural intuitive flow of ideas and creativity.

Learning to observe life without attachment to outcome takes you to a new level of freedom and mastery. It frees trapped energy to move in the direction of your desire. Letting go allows the universe to take over. That is when opportunities, events, and people show up to help you achieve your dream. You don't get to decide *how* this is to be accomplished. (That is the part that frustrates people.) You get to take action as it is mandated.

Imagine that you are on a raft in the river, flowing gently, and you give permission to the river to take you, to hold you, and to guide you. This is metaphor brings to mind your agreement to let the Universe take hold in your life and flow its energy through you. As you do this, you open a channel to greater creativity and learn to give up resistance as well. In other words, the universe knows the way and you don't (even if you think you do).

There is a principle in Taoism called *Wu Wei*, which literally means *non-action* or *non-doing*. In the *Tao Te Ching*, Lao Tzu explains that beings who are wholly in harmony with the Universe (*Tao*) behave in a completely natural, uncontrived way, which is the goal of spiritual practice. Effortless ease, as it is called, amounts to living in such a way as to submit to the universal energy working in your life. Another way to say this is that the universe sets up the situation and you make yourself available to it.

As you develop skill, you discover the simplicity of accomplishing results as the crow flies, i.e., in the most direct manner. To reach your objective with the least amount of effort and angst, the universe, in its great wisdom, knows the easiest way to move you from point A to point B. Thus, as you flow with the universe, you are supported and supplied. Each opportunity and person that is instrumental to accomplishing your purpose is placed before you. Your job is to respond and take necessary action. In so doing, you are moved from one step to the next, in the right order, to develop the qualities and characteristics needed for your ultimate arrival. It is like stepping across a creek from one stone to the next until you are safely on the other side.

We have all heard of rock stars and celebrities who had a hit song or movie and soared to the top of their profession, only to plummet because they could not handle all that went with fame. They ended up in precarious conditions, often succumbing to drugs, alcohol, or other ego gratifications.

They lost sight of the purpose of their gifts and the chance to share them.

The same thing can happen to any of us who do not take advantage of the challenges meted out as we flow with the river. Each situation and relationship advance your abilities to rise higher, to learn more, to succeed in endeavors in new and brilliant ways. That is why we are here. We eventually want to graduate earth life and live in the expanded energy of love full time.

Life is an adventure at best, and you get to learn amazing lessons and build strength as you traverse through it. Hence, learning to step back a bit in each new venue and ask, *"What is the purpose of this?"* helps you gain clarity, wisdom, and stature. Your vision will expand, and you will begin to understand the transient nature of your involvement. Each time you do this, your deepest intuitive connection gains strength.

You may have a dear friend and, at some point, that friend may leave to experience new adventures. You can love your time with that person while you have it, but if you hold on to it, decide it is to be forever, or that it is the end-all of end-alls, your attachment may turn love and friendship into anger and resentment. People look for someone or something to blame instead of realizing that everything in the material world is of short duration. Yet, the river is forever flowing.

Learning to *see* life from a higher perspective is a great asset in discovering the power of non-attachment. Again, what is the purpose of this event, of this person appearing in my life? What is the opportunity? It may be to help you to learn a particular skill, provide an answer, solve a problem, or aid in putting the puzzle pieces of your experience together in a new way.

This is what higher vision is all about. You stop letting ego attachment determine your reactions. You take a moment to move to your heart and listen to the instructions there. Spirit will always guide you and you can learn to listen.

You may love your house, but don't become so attached that it destroys you if something were to happen to it. There are lots of houses as there are lots of cars, job, friends, and opportunities.

Let's say you have a business you wish to build. Pay attention. There are people to meet who can help. There are classes to take and books to read and resources that will move you toward your goal with insight and ease. Even challenges offer a deeper commitment, a more powerful stance to live your values.

Nelson Mandela, the former President of South Africa, lived with his vision of a free country where each person had the right to cast one vote. He held to this view despite being imprisoned for twenty-five years as a criminal against the state where he spoke his truth.

During his imprisonment, he cleansed himself of anger and became an advocate for the other prisoners. He used his education as an attorney to help them. His ability to work from inner calmness increased. He grew as a person and a leader. After twenty-five years, the time was right for the people and the world to stand up to Apartheid, the system of discrimination where the minority whites ruled over majority blacks.

The moment was right for people to come together. The world exerted pressure in a way that impacted the financial systems. As a result, Mandela was finally released from prison, a new man. His election to the presidency followed and he proved himself to be a wise, benevolent, non-violent leader. The pieces of the puzzle came together. He was ready, the people were ready, and the world was ready.

When we view this story from the perspective of Spirit, everything that needed to happen, did happen. It resulted in a peaceful transfer of power because Nelson Mandela was adamantly against violence and for equality.

This is an example of how life works when we develop the power of non-attachment, along with effortless ease. It does not mean we aren't busy working on developing skills, learning and seeking opportunities, and managing the challenges of the moment, but we do this with the knowing that the universe has our back, that we are working in concert with Greater Intelligence. We trust this Intelligence and guidance.

A few years ago, the fellow who owns the building where my office is located came to me with a proposition. He said, *"Jean, I have good news and bad news."*

To which I followed, *"Okay, let's hear it. What is your good and bad news?"*

He informed me that the tenant next to my office needed more space, which dictated that I move my office. *"Would you be willing to do this?"*

I always recognize the universe at work in these situations. I responded, *"If I move, will you pay for my move and for the transfer of my phone, etc.? Can I choose the carpet and colors for my new office?"*

He responded affirmatively.

"Okay, let's see what you are offering." And off we went to check out the new office suite.

The back-story is that I have always had a picture in my mind of a beautiful office with a bank of windows. (I love windows.) The image has always been there as a mental picture and I never did anything to find it, as I was content with my office as it was.

This day, we walked down the hall to a corner office so the he could show me the proposed space. When I stepped into the new office suite, I saw two walls of windows. My heart leaped. *This is it.* I knew it.

We worked out the deal and I moved into my new suite. When I was unpacking, I found a list that I had written a year or two earlier. It was an affirmation that said, *My New Office: lots of windows, a certain amount of square footage, a storage closet, beautiful, peaceful, easy rent.* I had forgotten all about this list.

This new space was larger than anticipated in my affirmation. I now had lots of extra space and a small storage room. Did I say how much I love space? My rent remained the same as I paid before with my smaller suite. Whoo Hoo! The universe had blessed me again!

This is how these principles work. I was not attached to my office. I was willing to move with the universal River, and everything on my list was fulfilled in even better ways than imagined. When we meet this ease, it is definitely a sign that we are on track and cooperating with universal flow.

In Richard Bach's book, *Illusions,* he speaks of river creatures that spend their entire lives grasping the bank of the river. They are petrified of letting go, lest they die in the flow of the river. Yet, one such creature, out of sheer exhaustion, finally decided to release the riverbank. He was no longer willing to cling in desperation.

As he let go, the river lifted him into its flow and down the stream he went. In the process, he discovered new worlds. He ended his journey in a beautiful pond where there was abundant food and sunlight. He was home.

This is what happens when we let go. We are taken to greater opportunities, expanded experiences, the right people, and a fulfilled life.

The Dalai Lama, the spiritual leader of Tibet, illustrated the principles of non-attachment and non-judgment. He was asked, *"Why is it that you don't hate the Chinese for taking your country and killing and torturing your people?"*

He responded, *"It would be inefficient."*

The inefficiency of hatred is obvious. When you hate, you create a blockage in the flow of energy coming into and through your mind and body. You become locked down, torturing yourself. The love that is inside cannot be expressed. You are trapped while the person(s) you hate are as free as ever.

Energy requires free movement in order to function effectively and efficiently. Universal energy wants to flow through us. When it does, we are benefitted along with all we come in contact. And when we interfere with this free flow of energy, we diminish ourselves proportionately. We lose health, wealth, goodwill, joy, friendship, love, and opportunity.

It is as easy as deciding the kind of person you want to hang out with. Is it a positive, joy filled person or an angry one? Be the one you choose. We all want happy people in our lives. So, be one! Then you attract in like kind.

Blocking energy flow also results in illness and body discomfort. Sickness is a sign that we are out of alignment with Spirit. People will excuse their conditions with statements like, *"I am old."* That is nothing but an excuse. If it were the truth, every old person would have the same maladies, but they don't. The truth is that blocked energy creates physical debility. Period. Choose differently.

Having does not mean holding. One way we interfere with the free flow of energy is by holding on to what we already have. We hold on to money or other material things. We hold on to relationships past their expiration date. Attaching to events/experiences blocks the pleasure the original experience offered and inhibits the free movement of new things and new people into our lives.

Do you want the freedom of universal flow? If so, submit to it and stay open. You will have an amazing ride. Your job is to agree and allow. Pay attention. Good things are happening. Here we go!!!

Have you ever been told that you can't sell a house in December? That is what I was told.

But, fortunately, I didn't believe it. As a result, I sold my house in December and I purchased one in December. My belief was that there are people seeking housing every month of the year. There is no shortage – of buyers, of sellers, of houses. Thus, I sold my house.

The point is that, when we draw a conclusion that poses a lacking, unsupportive universe, we are limiting our experience. There is NO lack in the Universe. Whatever you need, it is available. In the housing market, there are people seeking houses in December, January, February, and every month of the year. I put my trust in the abundance of the universe above my trust in other people's opinions and beliefs, and the universe came through for me. It always does. Trusting the universe to function perfectly is the key to having the benefits of that perfection.

Cultivate your connection to the bounty and grace of the universe by doing the activities in this book. For every minute you apply to connection and openness and developing your intuitive knowing, you are paid volumes in ease and joy.

To reiterate, when we open to universal Energy and allow it to flow through us without resistance, it brings us to our next step and opportunity for growth. We essentially move our small egoic, fear-based self out of the way. When we drop the negative self-talk, opinions, and conclusions, we make room for brilliant ideas and resources to show up. Slowly, we recognize our amazing power and limitlessness.

The universe wants the best for each person. It has *no* prejudices or biases. It doesn't even register your ego identification. If you saw a child dressed up as a witch or a princess, you would know that she was playing with that identity. You would not be fooled in thinking that she is anything but a beautiful, glowing child underneath the garb. In the same way, God doesn't register your ego demeanor. God perceives his beautiful child in a glowing gown of Light. In the mind of God, you are his offspring, a bright Light in the world.

You are a cell in the body of the universe. You receive equal nourishment, joy, abundance, and grace as all other cells/beings. Only you, with a closed mind, can restrict this flow.

So, set your goals and trust that the Universe will help you to achieve them. To be effective in practicing the principle of non-attachment, you must believe that the universe is abundant. No matter what you desire, it is available and on its way to you. Through the law of magnetic attraction, what you focus on increases.

Keep your focus clear and allow the Greater Intelligence of the Universe to do its work. Just as in the story of Nelson Mandela, everything is moving into the right place and time to bring you what you want or even better.

Practice non-attachment by enjoying your home, your possessions, your work, friends, family, and at the same time, be willing to let go if the occasion arises. Each item has brought you blessings. What are they?

Each time I moved to a different house or office, or changed cars, or left behind a relationship, I took a minute to give thanks to a completed experience. - my old home, car, office, or relationship. Each item brought expansion and awareness.

Releasing with gratitude keeps you open for the next blessing. Soon you become a funnel for blessings. You flow naturally with the river of life, letting go of old beliefs, practices, superstitions, opinions, and material items as you go, ever ready for the next blessing, the next miracle, and a greater way to share and love. Life is amazing.

Activity

When you notice someone doing something that you wouldn't do, practice letting go of the need to judge that person. You can say to yourself; *I don't know what he is doing, but it is none of my business.*

That does not mean that, if a person is harming someone, you don't call the police. It means that you reserve judgment. You can speak the facts to the police.

Practice letting go of judgments in the following situations:

* You don't receive a phone call for which you have been
  waiting.
* You submit a purchase contract on a house you just love, and
  you find out that someone else got there first.
* You discover that a friend has been disloyal.
* You are in heavy traffic, running late for an appointment.

In each situation, the practice is to get *centered*, which means
to clear the slate of your mind. Focus on breathing and on knowing
that right-action is taking place, that there is a higher plan working
right now. Accept it. None of the above situations, nor others you
can imagine, preclude you from taking action. Just don't act out of a
sense of loss or panic. For instance, you can call someone and say,
"I'm stuck in traffic and will be late for the meeting." Do this
without judgment.

Pay attention to your intuitive instructions. What are your
urges and whisperings? Are you being guided to move in some
way? If so, do it. If not, listen daily for guidance.

Make a personal agreement: if something is not working, step
back, take a break, re-evaluate, try something different, or let go.

Enjoy everything. Hold on to nothing.

***

Become Non-Resistant

Becoming non-resistant to the flow of life, keeps your mind
open and soon you are able to see the purpose behind things that
previously you refused to consider. Life has its own way to move
you along your journey. To become non-resistant so that you can
arrive at your destination with the least number of bumps and
bruises (spiritually or physically), let go of the need to control
everything.

Often in our haughtiness, we think we know the best way to
accomplish everything. We certainly have been given a formula for
the perfect life. Education, good job (includes a 401K, health
insurance, vacation pay), marriage, children (at least 2), work until
retirement, and retire. This is our cultural/tribal program. Living it
without question can dull your senses and squash your creative

spirit because life/the universe might have a whole other way to bring you to your purpose.

Thus, becoming non-resistant means to let go of the way YOU think it should be, and listen deeply for the way it needs to be.

Have you ever asked for something and when an opportunity showed up to have what you requested, you stood back and said, *"No, thank you?"* I have seen this scenario many times. A woman asked Spirit for a loving soul mate. When such a man showed up, she ran. Why? Because she was not used to being loved. She had not learned to love herself. She continued to allow the voice of self-defeating criticism run her life and she remained in fear of being inadequate in a loving relationship. *"He will find out how unworthy I am and leave."* Thus, instead of honoring her desire, she ran from it. Interestingly, this phenomenon happens just as often to men as it does to women.

Another version of this scenario would be that, in not feeling worthy of a loving relationship, you do something to sabotage it. It is a way to keep something from yourself that you feel unworthy of having. If you think *you are not good enough*, you can sabotage a job you love, or having money, or owning a great home, or finding a trustworthy friendship, or doing anything fun.

You can ignore or avoid the efforts of the universe to respond to your needs and desires. In fact, resistance can block your reception of all gifts.

One of the ways you lose power is by resisting events and people. Resistance blocks the free flow of energy and movement. It keeps you stuck and denies pleasure. Most importantly, it keeps you focused in the ego, your critical voice, and not in your True Self, which is love. Resistance is based in fear (fear of the unknown) and keeps you small, needy, and unhappy.

You are in resistance when you have to be right, won't accept assistance, or remain closed to new ideas or methods of accomplishment. You resist when winning something becomes the most important factor - more important than anything else. You resist when you are unable to give or receive compliments, and when you blame. All of these behaviors create rigid energy in your body and mind. Muscular tightness is an easy way to spot the energy of resistance.

Often people avoid learning something new because they want to believe they know everything. Again, this reflects fear. To be afraid of a new way, idea, or possibility keeps you trapped in old, used experiences and dried up energy.

Resistance keeps you from expanding into the exalted being you are designed to be. The universe is ever pushing you to become your True Self. Flowing with it requires willingness to step into the unknown. As you proceed in unknown territory, you understand the underlying purpose of events and relationships that you may have previously resisted. It all makes sense.

It is important to know that you are always attracting the perfect situations, circumstances, and people to help you heal past misunderstandings and wounds. As these show up, you have a chance to learn and grow. Just being aware of this one fact can help you achieve the right perspective. We are always connected to a Greater Mind that efforts in our favor. When we resist the blessing of its guidance, we make life hard – a struggle.

I know a woman, Rochelle, who is angry with her employer, Herman. She's not angry because Herman has been mean to her, for she dearly loves him. Her anger comes from him being lied to by his daughter and him refusing to see it. The daughter, Susan, steals money from Herman's company and finagles the books to cover the losses, often leaving Herman in the lurch for money at important times. Yet, Herman seems oblivious to her actions.

As far as Herman is concerned, he is in denial about what is going on with his daughter because the pain of accepting her deceit would be too much for him. It's easier to look the other way.

On the other hand, the dishonesty and unfairness of the situation upsets Rochelle to the point where she becomes ill. Her enragement has much deeper roots than what appears on the surface. She is angry because the elements of the situation revert back to her former marriage where she was in a similar position as Herman. Her ex-husband lied and cheated, covering his tracks for years. Rochelle's resentment toward Susan's dishonesty is magnified because Rochelle has never forgiven her ex-husband for his philandering nor forgiven herself for accepting it. Each day, as she observes

Susan's tricks and deceit at work, her old wound is reopened and all the pain of the past floods back.

To create peace in her life, Rochelle must make the next move. She must forgive her former husband and let go of the past. If she doesn't, she will be dragging it with her wherever she goes, and it will be re-created again and again. Her wound will not heal until she allows it to heal. She must learn to live in the present and not in the past. Rochelle is the only one that can heal her pain and her heart.

Herman may think he is in happy oblivion by ignoring the problem, but he is resisting the truth about his daughter. Susan is in resistance because she is accumulating guilt and hatred toward herself for her dishonest behavior.

In this situation, each person is resisting life and blocking the flow of blessings from the universe. Rochelle wastes time trying to correct Herman's perceptions. Instead, she could be healing herself. Herman wants to believe his daughter is devoted and loving, so he lives in delusion. One day, he will have to face the deficiencies in his treasury. Susan's belief in lack is so strong that she feels she must steal to get ahead. She justifies and rationalizes her thievery, feeling guiltier and guiltier. And so, it goes. These individuals have planted seeds of dishonesty in their mental gardens.

They are all worthy of something much better, but none of them have claimed it.

Not loving yourself is the biggest and most common form of punishment. It keeps you in a prison of self-hatred and resistance. Often, people project their misunderstandings and misinterpretations onto others. The mind then gets busy judging and fixing everyone else, while the real work of correcting yourself is lost. This state of denial reflects the ease of looking outside for answers, instead of embracing your personal lessons.

Each person in Rochelle's story is obstructed and resistant to truth. Which person in the scenario did you relate to? Did you identify with any of the characters or the scenario?

Through the span of your life, you have formed false concepts regarding who you are and of what you are capable. To heal these misperceptions, you unknowingly draw people and circumstances to you so that you might deal with the matching energies. Each scenario reveals your erroneous thoughts, but also provides the opportunity to adjust and heal. By *seeing* with spiritual eyes, you can discover a higher meaning to these events and relationships.

An art therapist I know, Clarice, works in a psyche ward in a hospital. The patients are delusional, drug-addicted, criminally insane, and everything in between. All of them live in fear because their egos are in complete control. Their problems relate to unworthiness and fear. Clarice's job is to help them find peace and create balance. She also understands that these folks have been placed in her life to represent her own mental delusions of fear and unworthiness. This awareness keeps her lesson front and center in mind, and she knows that as she works with the patients, she is also helping herself.

The universe teaches us by offering mirrored circumstances to help us see what we have created through wrong thinking. These occasions often seem exaggerated, like with the mental hospital, but that also makes them easier to spot. Perhaps, we need drama to take notice.

The question for you is, *how is this situation to help me, bless me, teach me?* When you understand this mirror-effect and learn from it, you discover your own internal errors and grow in awareness. The answers are always available. Listen to your inner voice and it will keep you informed.

Clarice's opportunity is the same as yours and mine. She is to ask how she is reflected in the events and people in her job. What are they there to illustrate to her? What is the blessing in understanding these things? We always have a choice. We can learn while things are simple or wait until they become dramatic, chaotic, or desperate.

There are gifts being offered everywhere all the time, even in what might appear to be negative circumstances. When you are willing to adjust your view to see through the eyes of Spirit and release resistance, you will realize new meanings and discover the peace that is beyond understanding.

Another common scenario is an individual who was severely criticized and corrected as a child. He will draw to himself harsh, punitive people, be it spouse, friend, coach, or boss. All of these folks were also dealt with harshly, and so the cycle continues.

Severe judgmental attacks on others will persist because these folks continue to inwardly attack themselves. They get comfortable in harsh circumstances because they match their low self-esteem. It is when a person willingly looks within to heal their negative self-concept, will this cycle stop. Love is stronger than fear and criticism and judgment are projections of fear. As self-love evolves, a shift takes place and healing commences. In every situation of this type, there are doorways out. Pay attention and you will recognize the opportunity to move beyond negative self-judgment and harsh circumstances.

A minister tells a story about how he and his wife set out on a vacation. They decided to travel on their motorcycle. Hence, they mapped out their route on nice, smooth highways all the way to their southern destination. About a hundred miles into the trip, they ran into a detour. Orange cones stood across the road like plastic soldiers blocking their path. Next to the cones, a big, bright arrow pointed to different road. It was a gravel path.

"Yikes, traveling on gravel on a motorcycle is horrible!" the man lamented in distress. "This is not the way it is supposed to be. This is not how we planned it. It is not fair...."

The minister did not believe that the lesson they were to learn was to never take a vacation, nor was it about bad karma. He felt it was for him to decide how he was going to face adversity. Being too far from home and too near their destination to turn back, they slowly entered the gravel road in an effort to make the best of it. After a few hundred yards, the gravel road reverted back to a smooth highway.

For a moment, the minister had considered the idea of victimhood. *Bad luck. Not fair.* Then, he selected a more evolved approach. *This is how it is, so let's deal with it.* In choosing a positive reaction, he found peace.

What would you have chosen?

An important aspect to non-resistance is this: beneath every outer circumstance is a deeper meaning. For instance, many people deal with the ending of a relationship as a time of blame and recrimination. *Well, that person wasn't right for me anyway. That person didn't appreciate me or treat me right. It's his/her fault.*

When blame is your reaction, you are looking at appearances only. Beneath the seeming reality, something else is happening. The Universe is literally moving you to a greater lesson and opportunity. Most of the time, people miss the *real* lesson, because they are busy focusing on and protecting their ego. They hold a fear of looking bad or fear of being wrong.

There was a man who sold his business because he hit a dry patch and was fearful of not being able to make payroll. He was only looking at what appeared to be happening from a short-term perspective. Consequently, in his desperation, he sold the business to an unscrupulous buyer, who ended up trashing the business and suing the seller, implying that the seller had sold him a faulty product and was fraudulent in his pricing. The original business owner lost millions of dollars and his reputation was smudged. Later, he came to terms with certain factors: 1) He had sold his business out of fear, 2) he had noted some unscrupulous behaviors from the buyer early on, but was so focused on his need for money that he didn't stop the transaction, and 3) he should never act out of desperation.

The lesson was costly. Yet, the bottom line was that the original business owner learned from his situation and came back stronger. He chose to transcend fear and to pay close attention to his intuition in dealing with people. Ultimately, he learned to do business for the love of it and to work with people who had integrity. He turned away opportunities for quick cash where integrity and honor were not the focus. As he pursued his passion for building things, he recognized his power to magnetize opportunity to him. He could do this whenever he remembered the great talents and skills he was offering to his customers. He rebuilt his fortune. Through this transformational process, he had become a new person.

It is this underlying quality of growth we must look for as we deal with life experiences.

Janine was having major health problems. It started with Crohn's disease, then expanded to urinary incontinence and serious digestion problems. When I looked at Janine's body in a psychic reading, I found incredible a pattern of tightness and rigidity throughout. This pattern seemed to echo a mental mantra in Janine's mind: *I have to fix it. I have to fix everything.*

I asked Janine, *"What is it you have to fix?"*

She informed me that her husband, Jeffrey, was beside himself with the up-coming death of his dog, which had been his pal since childhood.

Psychically, I checked this out and saw that Jeffrey had made peace with his dog's terminal illness. He was ready to accept his pet's demise. He seemed to be managing his sorrow well.

Janine, on the other hand, was the one who was freaking out. Why... because she was not in control. She could not *fix* any of it. She couldn't fix the dog, or the illness. She couldn't prevent the dog's demise or interfere with her husband's sadness. The only thing she could control was herself and she was doing a terrible job at that.

So, the bottom line was that Janine was ruining her own health by living in resistance to the natural flow of life. She resisted because she wanted things to be a certain way, and they weren't.

She told me she was exhausted.

Well, of course she was. It takes tremendous energy to resist life. Every part of her mind and body was tight and unyielding. Would she end up losing her colon or have to have stomach or urinary tract surgery before she got the message? Let go! Let God!

This kind of resistance is a learned habit. Janine held the idea that everything had to be perfect all the time. And *perfect* meant *her* version of perfect.

I suggested that maybe everything was already perfect, and perhaps it was time for her to accept that. The opportunity for Janine is amazing. She can create personal freedom by letting go and bring peace into her life by accepting what is. Her situation is a gift. It offered potential for growth.

You, too, can look for growth in your life. You are continually offered lessons to build character, strength, and skills and potential to evolve. As you work with each lesson, you expand in consciousness. The Universe is constantly guiding you. It helps you meet the right people to assist in your evolution and amplify the characteristics you have come into this life to develop.

Examine your life now. Are you fighting life? Telltale signs are defensiveness, excuses, need for control, and the tightness you feel in your body. Who do you want to blame? In what way are you angry or resentful? This is how resistance reveals itself.

When you resist you bar Spirit from entering your mind and life. You are saying, *"I want to be in control, and I am not willing to be open to a greater way."*

Water flows downhill, around tree stumps, and over rocks. Life flows in this way also. The stream trickles down the mountain. The wind blows where it will. Waves roll freely to shore. The seasons flow, one to the other. And so it is with life. This free flow of energy exemplifies our natural state. This is Spirit. It carries change easily, subtly, and effortlessly. We are to honor and trust this flow. As we recognize change as a natural occurrence, we allow it its due without resistance.

These are signs of resistance. Do you recognize any?

- Blaming others for your circumstances
- Anger
- Taking things, events, remarks, or actions personally
- Always in a hurry
- Trying to make others happy
- Trying to make your children into what you want them to be
- Stubbornly holding to your agenda when everything points to a different way

When you stop fighting life, it is easy to accept mean-spirited folks for who they are: wounded. And the truth is, their unhappiness has nothing to do with you.

You can *choose* how you feel with each event. In every example, you can choose to remain peaceful, to wait patiently, or be willing to see the Universe working *for* you. When you do that, you remain connected to Spirit and Joy and you develop knowing.

Activity

Pay attention to your body and notice restriction. Mentally note what you are resisting. (Change, being wrong, accepting someone or something, whatever?)

Your body will tell you by the pressure or rigidity you feel.
Notice your reactions to events and people.
Observe judgments and resistance in yourself.
Discern when you want to fight, to be right, compete for the last word, or you have to win.
When you discover these barriers, relax and breathe.
Observe your anger and resentment. They will help you recognize victimhood. If you notice yourself being a victim, decide if that is the mental state you want to experience.
Mark when you want to complain or feel helpless. Step back and decide if you are being honest. Are you really helpless? If not, do something to change things.
You will experience times when you are not focused in you core Spirit – This awareness activity will help you pay attention and release resistance.
Scan yourself daily and make a habit of letting go. Soon you fill find more energy pouring through your body and mind.
Relax into breathing and let go. Make this your default activity

when life seems to get serious.

***

Forgiveness is the Key to Peace

In our fear-based world we have learned to take everything personally and fault others for our circumstances. As a result, we live wounded lives and carry toxic beliefs and energy that block our connection to Spirit. Learning to forgive (yourself first) brings you back to the reality that you are in charge of your life. Forgiveness releases pain, heals wounds, and paves the way to deeper spiritual connection. It opens the door to peace and knowingness. You were not put on the earth to be perfect by material or cultural standards. You already are perfect as a spiritual being. Focusing on perfection as a human being is wasteful, inefficient, and distracting. By concentrating on your real work, you see beyond the small hurts of the ego. Hence forgiveness becomes natural. Your goal is connection to your Greater Self and anything that keeps you from it is too big a price to pay. That is why Jesus said, *"Forgive them for they know not what they do."* People who do harmful things and make mean-spirited statements don't know any better. They are like children who have not been taught better. Forgive them. Your goal is too important to carry around pain from unevolved, wounded beings.

Mahatma Gandhi made an important point when he stated, *The weak can never forgive. Forgiveness is the attribute of the strong.* We want to be strong in forgiveness because it is the key to living a peaceful life.

Many people confuse forgiveness with condoning, but that is not correct. You can let go of a grievance without condoning negative behavior. People have their own reasons for being ruthless, greedy, angry, and resentful. None of this has anything to do with you. Everyone operates from his own state of consciousness, with his memories and values. It is what makes spiritual progress an individual matter.

Because of the ornery nature of the ego, the undisciplined man is uncomfortable, even mean-spirited, toward those who are different from him. Exalted masters train their followers to stay even-tempered, without shock or intimidation, by materially minded folks who do not understand the path of the spiritual devotee.

Jesus instructed his followers that when they were reviled or made fun of because they walked a different walk, they were to take no heed, for they were blessed in Heaven. It was clear to him that there are many people who are not ready to separate themselves from their physical, egoic desires to experience the higher energy of spiritual love. He told them that when they entered a town and were not received, to shake the dust from their sandals and move on.

The story of the Gerasene demoniac in the Bible illustrates the dynamics of a group of people turning away from that which would heal. As the story goes, Jesus and his disciples docked their boat in the territory of Gerasene and, forthwith, Jesus healed a demoniac man who had been chained in a cemetery. The chain represents the man's mind attachment to the past, which resulted in insanity. (Maybe you relate??)

The man had many demons, which reflected divergent painful memories and numerous emotional wounds. Jesus healed the man by casting out his insane thoughts: anger, resentment, guilt, shame, and grief. Against the instructions of Jesus, the man went into town and informed the people of his incredible recovery. As a result, the town's people, rather than welcoming

Jesus went to him and asked him to leave their territory.

This story perfectly depicts the demented mental attitudes of people wanting to remain in a disillusioned state rather than permitting the light of peace and love to enter, cleanse, and bring healing to them. There are many who do not understand or acknowledge spiritual practices or who are intimidated by those who actively pursue growth. Nonetheless, others' concerns of that nature need and be of no consequence to the seeker.

The Bible tells us that they are blessed who are reviled and persecuted and falsely spoken against. By living in the highest energy of love, a person can become impervious to negativity, just as Jesus did not take on the hatred and fear of his captors. That kind of resilience is the testament to an exalted being and as such, this person is continually blessed.

No matter what comes at you in this world, you can maintain your stance in goodness, peace, mercy, compassion, and love. By so doing, you are blessed in Spirit. You are elevated beyond the illusion of ego and beyond right and wrong to the greater reward of spiritual oneness with God.

The Kingdom of Heaven can only be experienced with an open heart. Those who would cause harm to you or anyone are wounded beings. They project their pain onto others. Their minds have been twisted by misunderstanding and egoic interpretations.

If these kinds of individuals are present in your world, they are part of your healing and you are part of theirs. You bring healing to both by forgiving them, *for they know not what they do.* They are living in their wounds and projecting their painful reality to external events and people. They are afraid and have closed themselves off to warmth and nurturing. Their walls of distrust have grown thick. You, as a vessel of love, must see beyond their pain and refuse to participate in it.

As you make this decision, you pull away from the drama of victimhood. It is not relevant to you. As you disengage from negative ideas, the illusion of hatred dissolves and you are set free. In your attainment of freedom, you open a doorway to peace for you and the other, if he would have it.

Within the mental framework of forgiveness, you embrace the light within, which is the truth of your being. You recognize that, no matter the peril or challenge, your dedication is to live in peace, not letting the low energy of anger or hate intrude on your mental space. That is the way you align with the peace that passes understanding, the peace of God. In other words, you elevate your energy to align with God.

No matter what promise the temptation of revenge holds, it always results in sorrow. You cannot experience peace while you hold grudges, attack thoughts, or guilt over what you did or did not do. All are released as you hand these dark thoughts to Spirit. That is the meaning of the story of the Gerasene Demoniac.

During the Rwanda genocide in the mid-Nineties, Ilibagiza's entire family was brutally murdered. She managed to escape along with seven other women by hiding in a small bathroom during the horrific event.

Ilibagiza chose to forgive the people behind the death of her family because she knew that holding bitterness and anger would eventually destroy her. She wanted to bring something positive out of the horrendous experience. As a result, she wrote a best-selling book called, *Left to Tell,* and founded a charitable fund to help orphaned children who survived the genocide.

This was her healing.

The soul craves peace. Let that be your intention. No matter how rocky the path you walk, you will achieve it with undaunted patience and resolute determination. By merging your consciousness to love, you will attain the kingdom of Heaven.

The act of forgiving has multi-purposes. When you forgive an attack, you release a mental image that would otherwise hold you hostage. You open space in your mind for new life to enter. When you hold onto negative feelings and associations, you direct your life toward more of the same, which leads to an unfortunate future. Besides retaining a victim consciousness, you use an upsetting story as a template for more of the same kind of experience to enter your life. It is like handing your life over to the devil, if there were such a thing. In other words, you cannot experience beauty in the present moment when you hold on to negative imagery of the past.

Another story that illustrates forgiveness occurred in a small logging town in Oregon.

During World War II, a Japanese soldier named Nobus Fujita bombed the coastal forest range in Oregon. After the war, Fujita felt remorse and returned to Brooking, the small town near the surrounding forests he had bombed, to ask for forgiveness. To illustrate his regret and plea for forgiveness, he presented the town with a 400-year-old samurai sword that had been handed down in his family for generations. The town forgave him, hung the sword in the public library, and pronounced Fujita an Ambassador of Good Will.

Forgiveness is about cleansing your mental state so that the energy of love can enter. If your thinking is obsessed with past grievances, there is no space for love or peace. It is like taking poison and expecting someone else to die. Anger, resentment, and hateful thoughts are toxic. If they are your thoughts, you are the one who suffers. It doesn't matter what person you direct those thoughts toward. You still get the repercussions.

Consider your mind a blank screen and place upon that screen the things that have meaning for you, the things you choose to give energy to. If the scene you create is pastoral, you will feel peaceful. If what dominates your thoughts is negative, you will feel frustrated and chaotic. If you put vengeance and anger on the screen, you will find your life dark and unfriendly. Just as Ilibagiza realized, dark emotions would eventually destroy her.

The desire and longing for peace has to outweigh any momentary pleasure for revenge. To establish the mind in peace and grace, one must set aside humanity's need to win or to be right and to look to a greater reward of spiritual connection. Persistence in taking the high road of love will yield bliss.

Purity of the heart gives one contact with God.

The yogi who has completely calmed the mind and controlled the passions and freed them from all impurities and who is one with Spirit – verily, he has attained supreme blessedness.

Bhagavad Gita

Activity

Here is a forgiveness technique to follow in order to achieve a peaceful mind when it appears there has been a grievous act performed against you, or even if you have held a grievous thought against someone else. This technique dates back to ancient cultures, including the original Hawaiians.

Envision in your mind the person with whom you wish to make peace.

Speak to the person from the level of spiritual love saying:

I love you.
I forgive you.
Please forgive me.
Thank you.

Continue this process until you feel peace. As you release each egoic need to be angry, peace will flood your consciousness and you will be able to release the person and incident as though it never happened. On your slate and in your world, it didn't happen because you have wiped the energy of disharmony from your mind screen.

In this process, you are asking for forgiveness because you have chosen, on some level, to participate in the drama. You are thanking Spirit for the opportunity to be cleansed of the disrupted energy created by your ego while engaged in the drama.

VII. Trust

> Love is everything. It is the key to life, and its influences are those that move the world.
> Ralph Waldo Emerson

Understanding Energy

Summary:

Do you believe the Universe (God) loves you? Do you understand that you can live a charmed life? In this chapter, you will come to terms with the universe as a field of energy not unlike play-doe. You live in this universal energy and you are made of it. Seeing clearly helps you realize that the universe is without personality or judgment. In other words, you are always loved. When you comprehend the nature of the universe, which means understanding energy, you discover that it is always working to elevate your experience and bring your desired results.

Knowing who you are is part of the process. In the beginning was the light and all was created from that substance. Thus, the basis of all energy and life is light. It is the Universal substance out of which all things are made. Discovering this element as your Spiritual (inner state of being), frees you to operate with love, openness and trust, leaving behind guilt, shame, and anger.

Magnetism is a form of hypnosis and learning to use it as a tool for your betterment is important. We have been magnetized into believing outrageous things like, you are not good enough. Ha! The information in this section will set you free to use magnetism to replace false beliefs handed to you as a child and elevate your energy to live as an exalted being.
Once you understand how magnetism works, you can increase your magnetic attraction and your wishes cannot be denied. Magnetism is a tool to raise your energy and merge with your highest self. Understanding this principle increases self-trust and your ability to know truth.

***

Many people feel that the universe works in a random, happenstance way, that things don't happen according to a plan, and there isn't a way to comprehend how things evolve. But that is not true. The universe works according to certain, definite principles and by understanding these principles, we can shape our lives in the manner we choose. The first thing to recon with is that everything, from a table to a book, to a thought, is a form of energy. This premise makes understanding energy possible, even powerful. By understanding the nature of energy, you step into the power to manifest your objectives.

From a drop of water to a massive oak tree, everything is comprised of energy. By stepping back to recognize the inherent make-up of all things, you realize the transience of the material world and the stability of your inner world. In this section you will learn how to develop the mental discipline to direct energy toward your desired objectives.

When you understand energy, you can see beyond the material essence of things to the higher dimension of spirit. You are spirit first. These next sections will cast light on the nature of energy and how to direct your mind to experience Highest Energy.

***

You Are the Light

When you know who you are, you cannot be offended or deluded. Living in the world, not taking anything personally, and refusal to be offended sets you free. Many people live their whole life in a state of angst because they are put off and offended by other people. Being upset and perpetually angry is a terrible state. It keeps you off balance and unable to think clearly or address issues. You are certainly not strategic. In this chapter you will get clear on your True
Identity because YOU are the light.
In the beginning was the light and all was created from that substance. Thus, the basis of all energy and life is light. It is the universal substance out of which all things are made. As you discover this element as your Inner state of being, you will be freed

to operate with love, openness and trust, leaving behind guilt, shame, and anger. Indeed, you are the light. You have the ability to radiate and illuminate your world and live in the high state of Knowingness.

There are many near-death experiences reported wherein the individual describes an event of encountering a beautiful, warm, loving light.

For instance, Robin Michelle Halberdier of Texas City, Texas, illustrates the overwhelming sense of love she met as she experienced this light. Her near-death episode took place in a hospital when she was between one and two months of age. Born prematurely, she suffered from Hyaline Membrane disease and was not expected to live. In *Beyond the Light*, this is how she tells her story.

My first visual memory was looking forward and seeing a brilliant bright light, almost like looking directly at the sun. The strange thing was that I could see my feet in front of me, as if I were floating upward in a vertical position. I do not remember passing through a tunnel or anything like that, just floating in the beautiful light. A tremendous amount of warmth and love came from the light.

She describes a figure standing in the light. It was in the shape of a human, but without distinct facial features. It seemed masculine. The light emanated from the figure. Light rays shone all around him. Robin felt protected and safe and loved.

The figure in the light told me through what I now know to be mental telepathy that I must go back, that it was not time for me to come here. I wanted to stay because I felt so full of joy and peace. The voice repeated that it wasn't my time; I had a purpose to fulfill and I could come back after I completed it.

Robin told her parents about her encounter right after she began to talk. At the time, she believed that everyone had the same experience.

I told my mom and dad about the big glass case I was in after I was born, and the figure in the light and what he said to me. They took my reference to the glass case to mean the incubator. My mom told me this all of these years later when I brought the subject up again.

Robin began attending church at the age of five. She would look at the picture of Jesus and tell her mother that he was the one in the light.

There are many similar stories available in books and on the Internet. The point is that the light is real and is available to everyone if we are willing to see with different eyes. It is with our mental or intuitive eyes that we will see the Light. I have seen it since I was a child.

The practice of meditation is a great way for you to rediscover the light. As already said, you will not find it with your physical eyes. The dense material of your eyes is not designed to register such fine energy. But you can perceive the light with your mind. Because the inner light vibrates at a high frequency, it is discernible only with the fine mechanism of your mind.

In the Bible, (in Genesis) when God proclaimed, "*Let there be light*," light was created. Out of this primordial substance, all things were created, and that includes you.

Renowned physicist, Albert Einstein, determined that if you were to peer into a high-powered microscope and look deep into any physical item, past the electrons, protons, quarks, and atoms, you would discover light. He verified that everything in our physical universe is constructed from this primal element. That means it is everywhere in all things and everyone. It is our elemental substance.

This is the same light that people who go through near-death experiences report seeing. This high-resonating light is brilliant beyond imagination and deeply loving. When we exit the material world, we return to this original element. Yet, we don't have to expire to behold the phenomenon of inner light.

This light energy is subtle, still, and made up of the finest, highest vibratory energy. Even though you cannot see it with your eyes, you can feel it and sense it. You can reconnect with it by looking within, as in meditation.

Material forms, including bodies, are heavy and vibrate at a low frequency. Even though your physical eyes, also vibrating at a low frequency, cannot register the inner light, you may be able to perceive a subtle white light around these forms as a kind of halo. Your eyes can register but a narrow frequency of energy as it equates to the material world. Nevertheless, the light is ever-present and within reach, and you can align your mind to it. As you set your intention to return to the experience of light, your source, you are renewed.

Benjamin Breedlove experienced the light as a young boy. All his life, he experienced a heart condition that set a high risk of sudden death. During school one day, Benjamin collapsed, and his heart stopped beating for three minutes. He recovered and decided to make a video called *This Is My Life,* where he told his story. He used cards as an aid in his video.

One of the cards read that, even though he wasn't breathing, he heard people around him talking.

"He's not breathing. His heart has stopped, and he has no pulse."

Ben then experienced a white light and a feeling of peace. He said he was in a place that he didn't want to leave. However, he did wake up again on the floor.

At the conclusion of the video, Ben said, *"Do you believe in Angels or God? I do."*

A week after making his video and posting it online, Ben's heart failed.

The light is real and often people in vulnerable conditions will see it. My belief is that, because of their openness, these people drop all restrictions and identification with the material world and the high frequency of love draws them inward. For each one, it is an answer and a comfort.

In telling his story and making his video, Ben may have assuaged fear and offered reassurances that death simply brings us back home to the light.

***

Magnetize to your Higher Energy

Magnetism is a form of hypnosis. You can easily be magnetized into believing outrageous things like, *"You are not good enough."* Ha! The information in this chapter will set you free to learn how to use magnetism and how to replace beliefs handed to you through magnetism.

We are spiritual beings having a human experience and, as such, part of our power is in magnetism. We use this power every day. But do we use it to our betterment? Once we understand how magnetism works, we can increase our magnetic attraction and our wishes cannot be denied. Magnetism is a tool to raise your energy and merge with your Highest Self.

Understanding the principle of magnetism will increase self-trust and your ability to Know truth.

Did you know that you are a magnet? Magnetism is one of the prime moving forces in the universe. Magnetism binds the galaxies together and provides the power to transport the tiniest subatomic particles in your body. Napoleon Hill describes how magnetism works. *Our brains become magnetized with the dominating thoughts which we hold in our minds, and by means with which no man is familiar, these "magnets" attract to us the forces, the people, the circumstances of life which harmonize with the nature of our dominating thoughts.*

Around every magnet is an invisible energy field of attraction. For example, when a nail contacts a magnet, it is drawn, attracted, pulled to the magnet. The nail has no choice. It cannot ignore the magnetic field.

An interesting thing occurs when a nail connects with a permanent magnet. The nail becomes a temporary magnet itself. As a magnet, it acquires the ability to also attract, and as long as the nail remains near the permanent magnet, it retains its magnetic power. If the nail is moved, it returns to its original state and loses its attracting abilities.

There are scientific reasons for this. The atoms of the nail possess latent magnetic qualities, but they are disorganized. The atoms point in various directions and cancel out each other's electromagnetic charge. (Like people who don't know what they want or where they are going. Nothing happens for them.)

Contrarily, the atoms of a magnet are aligned. Their north and south poles face in the same direction. Therefore, when a magnet attracts a nail, the atoms of the nail line up to match the magnet. (The nail now has direction.) The nail emulates or copies the magnet. In so doing, it becomes a magnet, too. As long as it is aligned with the original magnet, it possesses magnetic qualities.

Taking this further, your physical body is a field of electromagnetic activity. Magnetic energy exists within the trillions of atoms that make up your body. You are a living, breathing, moving being of magnetic power. That is why you attract the things you focus on, whether or not you like them, want them, or despise them. You attract the things you hold dominant in your mind. The more aligned you are with your desires, good or bad, the more powerfully you will attract those things into your life.

Now, you are getting the idea that when you are congruent with a desire, it has no alternative but to be drawn to you. To be congruent means that you not only hold a thought in your mind, you feel it, breathe it, identify with it, and, in no way, contradict it. The thought itself is irrelevant. It is the congruency and alignment that matter.

People who are aligned are like magnets to other people. When you are around a person who is congruent or aligned, that person's magnetic power affects you. Also, the more congruent you are, the more charismatic you become. Your magnetic field expands, and you become irresistible to others. When Martin Luther King, Jr. gave his *I-have-a-dream* speech, he brought the whole crowd of listeners into his dream. Indeed, it became their dream. Because of his charisma and magnetism, he made his dream real for everyone.

John F. Kennedy was magnetic when he proclaimed, *"Ask not what your country can do for you but what you can do for your country."* He started a movement with that statement.

South Africans Bishop Desmond Tutu and Nelson Mandela have been great charismatic leaders and attracted millions of followers. It was through their efforts that Apartheid ended and all citizens received a vote. These men were unequivocal in holding to their beliefs. Neither waivered and as a result they created strong magnetism.

Of course, there are negative examples. Adolph Hitler spoke to the German people about a "pure race." They were humbled from losing world war one and used to having dominant leaders. As a result, he was able to use his personal magnetism and powerful message to lead them to great destruction.

From these examples, you can see why some people are leaders (magnets) and others are followers. Followers have not activated their magnetic power. They have not aligned with one desire or purpose. They have not realized who they are. They are like the nail without the powerful force of the magnet: atoms in disarray.

If you really want to achieve something, align with it. Speak it, walk it, talk it, feel it, think about it, and take action. Your desire cannot say "No" to you. Through the principle of magnetism, the opportunity to have what you want will be drawn to you. When you hold this truth, the necessary idea or action will occur to you and you will realize your desire.

Activity

Pick individuals you admire and study their thought processes, behaviors, speech patterns, actions, ideals, etc. Begin to mimic their qualities. Start with their attitudes. Perhaps you can use their manner of speaking or their ideals. The idea is to allow their energy to magnetize the same qualities in you. If you admire certain individuals, you already have the same qualities in you that you admire in them. Use this exercise to bring out the qualities in you that you appreciate in others.

Elvis Presley loved the way the patrons sang at a southern gospel church. He attended their services and sang with them. It was by mimicking the qualities he admired that he became the *"King of Rock and Roll."* We all do this. The point is to make sure you are mimicking the actions and people who bring you to your highest good.

***

Trust the Universe

Do you have doubts about your place in the universe? Do you believe the universe (God) loves you? Do you know that you can live a charmed life? In this section you will come to terms with the universe as a field of energy not unlike play-doe or silly putty. In other words, it is moldable energy that easily succumbs to your vision.

We live in and are of the universe as a wave is in and of the ocean. We can mold our thoughts into manifested outcomes once we understand the nature and make-up of the universe. It really is without personality or judgment and does not work from the past, which means at any moment you can change direction and assume a new life.

This section acquaints you with the nature of the universe. As you become aware of its workings, you realize that it is always moving to elevate your experience. Thus, learning to trust the universe is key to developing inner knowing.

Every reality you wish to experience has a certain feeling, vibration, and energy. Health feels different from illness and prosperity vibrates quite unlike poverty. Happiness has a completely different feeling than sadness or depression. Figure out what it feels like to have already achieved what you want, and it can be yours. Jesus taught his followers to pray as though it was already done. In other words, live in the reality (knowing) of your completed outcome or intention. As you do this, you draw the fabric and energy to your ideal, and the material expression of it is assured.

Creating the material outcome you desire takes practice because it is the opposite of what the world teaches. Our culture instructs that life is happenstance; that there is no rhyme or reason to what happens in your life. *"Some people are popular and successful and other have been dealt a losing hand."* This is a recipe for victimhood.

The world states that your experiences create what you think and feel, that you are just a reactor. Yet, the opposite is true.

You are at the helm of your life adventure. You get to decide what you want to experience and how you want to feel about it. Instead of reacting to events from some habitual pattern that arose from your family dynamics, you can choose a different path.

In this section, we will examine the laws of the universe. Imagine that you are stuck in a project with a stringent deadline that is coming up quickly. Add to the scenario the fact that you are sleep-deprived and not eating well. All factors are working against you in completing your project within the given deadline. On top of that, you generate thoughts such as, *I'm in big trouble. I'll never make it. What if I get demoted or lose my job?*

Your nervous system goes into panic mode. Fear takes over and freezes your mind and your body becomes tense. Under these circumstances, it is impossible to connect with your creative mind. When lost in fear, you cannot find a satisfying solution.

Be aware that you live and breathe in a field of energy called the Quantum Field, which has the characteristic of being formed and shaped like clay. It is impressionable. Without knowing it, you are imprinting fear into this field. Feeling fear and vibrating to fear results in you being in trouble. In this case, you don't make your deadline. You might be demoted or
fired.

The outcome was predictable because it reflected your thoughts. It was your declaration. You thought it; you created it. The law of cause and effect was activated. The vibratory energy of fear had concluded with a negative result from the projection and creation of your negative thoughts. You manifested your beliefs.

If you were to contemplate the law of cause and effect along with the law of possibilities, you would have realized that there were multiple outcomes or probabilities for the same situation. You might have asked for help or requested a different deadline. You might have taken a break to rest and fuel your body or taken a walk to clear your mind. You might have decided that there was a way to accomplish your objective, meditating and opening your mind to answers that could have come through to you intuitively. These are a few potentials.

Each would have changed the outcome of your challenge.

The scientists Elmer F. Gates and Thomas A. Edison had specific techniques they used when stuck in a project. They let go and rested in order to stay open to receive the answers they sought.

Sitting in a quiet room, Gates waited for his answer to appear in his mind. Edison took a nap on the cot he kept in his laboratory when he was baffled with a project. He programmed his mind to present his solution when he woke from his nap.

The mind is a magnificent tool, and its power is without limit. If you narrow your focus to negative possibilities, you will never experience the breadth and depth of the brilliance available. Those who keep their minds open to possibilities, accomplish great things.

Nikola Tesla, a mechanical and electrical engineer and inventor, was considered a futurist. He is best known for his contributions to the design of the alternating electrical supply system and the rotating magnetic field. He stated: *The progressive development of man is vitally dependent on invention. It is the most important product of his creative brain. Its ultimate purpose is the complete mastery of mind over the material world, the harnessing of the forces of nature to human needs.*

Per his description, one day Tesla was walking and reciting poetry when an idea came like a flash of lightning. In an instant, the truth was revealed. *I drew with a stick on the sand the diagrams shown six years later in my address before the American Institute of Electrical Engineers, and my companions understood them perfectly. The images I saw were wonderfully sharp and clear and had the solidity of metal and stone, so much so that I told them, "See my motor here; watch me reverse it."* He was deeply moved to see his invention come alive.

Throughout his life, Tesla set himself apart from others because he always believed he was privy to greatness. His purpose was invention, and he maintained that as his focus to great sacrifice of a personal life. Tesla's belief, focus, and dedication served as *cause*, and his amazing creative contributions to design were the *effect*.

Tesla was right in separating himself from others, as he did not want to be the victim of anyone's limited ideas. To keep his brilliant mind performing required accepting the limitlessness of the mind and the field of intelligence in which he operated.

Actor, Jim Carrey began his career as a comedian when he was fifteen years old. By sixteen, he was making his living performing the opening acts for the successful comedians Buddy Hackett and Rodney Dangerfield.

However, Carrey had bigger dreams. He understood the power of the universe when he wrote a check to himself for seven million dollars *for services rendered.* He stuck the check in his wallet and looked at it every time he opened his wallet. Seeing the check reminded him that he was on his way to movie stardom.

One day, he got a call from a movie producer and was hired to star in a movie that paid him seven million dollars. Since then, he has been featured in many movies: *The Mask, Dumb and Dumber, Ace Ventura, When Nature calls, Batman Forever, The Cable Guy,* to name a few.

In 1998, he played a dramatic role in *The Truman Show* and won a Golden Globe Award for Best Actor. Later, he won a second Golden Globe Award. Since then, he has become one of the highest paid actors in Hollywood, with a reported asking price of $20 million per movie.

Carrey knew that writing the check and placing it in his wallet was seeding the universe for future fame and profitability. He trusted they universe to come through for him and it did.

Sid Bernstein worked in the entertainment business in New York. He took a course from the famous journalist, Max Lerner, and was required to read a foreign newspaper every week. Bernstein read a London paper and saw a small article about a British rock group. The next week, there appeared a bigger article about this same group. The third week, an even bigger article emerged. These articles propelled Bernstein to make several phone calls to London, which were followed by setting up business contacts. Out of this action, Bernstein got the rights to produce the first United States tour of the Beatles. The rest is history. He opened the field of possibilities by looking for opportunities and taking follow-up action. Anyone can do the same thing.

We can simplify the concept of cause and effect. Imagine dropping a wad of paper. It falls to the floor. The cause is dropping the paper and the effect is the paper hitting the floor. Or, you may walk into a room and smile at people. The people in the room smile back and many may even want to make a connection with you. This could lead to new friends. Or, perhaps you depart late for an important meeting without considering the heavy traffic and you end up being late. The cause? Leaving late. The effect? Being late.

We live in an orderly universe, governed by distinct, definite laws. Whenever we succeed, it is because we are living in alignment with those laws. If we expect brilliance and set up the right environment to experience it, we achieve brilliance. When we do not succeed, we are not living in alignment with those laws. In other words, we set up the circumstances to be late, even when what we want is to be on time. It is that simple.

What causes have you set up in your life? Would you like to change them? If so, how?

Are you willing to stay open to ideas that will lead you to a greater result?

Drifting along on a sailboat is a great metaphor for flowing along easily in life. There are other comparisons between life and sailing. For instance, when you have your sail set, which represents having your goal established, the wind passes through the sails and creates a vacuum, which represents the need for your skills, your product, or your vision. In sailing, it is the vacuum that pulls the boat forward. Setting the sails in this way serves as an efficient use of wind. By the same token, it is the need for your product or service, along with your willingness to be available to meet those requirements that will pull you forward in business.

Think of yourself as the sailboat and the universe is represented by the wind and ocean. You are sailing or flowing with the universe and the currents of the time in which you live. The universe is ever your guide, and your job is to pay attention as you are directed.

Each time period has requirements. These can be identified and creatively met. In other words, creative people pay attention and develop the explicit products that meet the needs of the world at that precise time. It is called, *"going with the flow"* or letting the vacuum, the need of the moment, pull you forward. Remember the saying, *Necessity is the mother of invention. Hence, the airplane, electric toothbrush, microwave, self-cleaning oven, cell phone, internet, websites, etcetera.*

After World War II, there was an instant need for affordable housing for the returning soldiers. The people who met this need not only met a real, tangible requirement of the times, but made a lot of money as well. The same can be said of the developers of the light bulb, the airplane, the computer, the microwave, the cell phone, and wash-and-wear clothing. Each inventor was tuned to the times and found a way to fulfill the present needs.

There is another position in sailing called the Beam Reach, where the sail is set perpendicular to the wind so that the wind pushes the boat. This is the slowest method to propel the boat forward. This technique compares to people who resist life. When everyone is going north, the resistor wants to go south. When the whole team is working together, the dissenter wants to take a solitary approach.

It's a choice to flow with or resist life. When you flow, you take advantage of opportunities and tailor your talents to meet the needs. When you resist the flow, you block energy. That could be like living in the past and preventing yourself from moving forward when the times demand it. In that case, you miss out on the moment. That would be like a buggy whip company continuing to manufacture buggy whips when everyone has gone to driving cars.

To develop a strong sense of knowing be aware of the workings of the universe. Everything can be known ahead of time by paying attention. The universe is always informing of what is coming up next. There are signs and symbols all over the place. The airplane fulfilled the need of getting to your location quickly. The microwave was crucial in getting dinner on the table fast. With the cell phone you could call or text anyone, anywhere in seconds. You can see that fast movement is the sign of the times we live in.

The key is to trust the ebb and flow of life. Is there a way to set your sails for greater efficiency while working with the winds of change? The universe has your back. It is always sending signals for the next step. How might you trust the forces moving you forward now?

Activity

As you meet and talk with people, see beyond their faces to the beauty of their spiritual essence. Try to see the light within each person. What unique qualities do each express?

Register them.

As you listen to others, give your complete attention. Acknowledge them and offer your energy in return.

Notice if there is a message for you in the give-and-take. Each interaction is a divine moment, and there are messages everywhere. See if you can detect the universe at work in each moment. Tune in as best you can and your knowing faculty will get stronger.

VIII. Putting It All Together

Inherently, each one of us has the substance within to achieve whatever our goals and dreams define. What is missing from each of us is the training, education, knowledge, and insight to utilize what we already have.

Mark Twain, Author

Summary:

This section is about lifting the mind through gratitude and service. Gratitude keeps you in highest energy and service is love in action. You need these soft, nurturing qualities to fully embrace your spirit and realize your ultimate potential.

Gratitude and service bring you to your heart and that is where inner connection occurs.

As you engage in them, your inner knowing gets stronger

It is said that the happiest people are the ones who serve others. There is a reason for that. Service is the way you set the ego aside and rise to soul fulfillment. To take a break from your personal needs and recognize that the world needs you is humbling and rewarding at the same time. Service expands your energy, validates your gifts, and moves you to highest expression. Service, accomplished with right intention, connects you to your highest consciousness and intuition.

The desire to serve, to make a difference, is the natural outcome of the transformation you are making. You are moving beyond the ego to your true self of connection.

The last part of this section outlines a suggested daily action plan. Putting the principles into play in your life guarantees the results you seek. Use this plan or create one of your own.

Either way, take steps daily to build a powerful connection to your inner voice of intuition.

The world is your playground. You get to decide and be whatever you want. Intuition is your guide. By developing your power and potential every possibility exists. There is a higher (finer) way to live life. By practicing the principles in this book, you can raise your energy at will. This automatically ignites passion and joy. You feel great. Everything is possible, available and fun. Connection to your Higher Consciousness is the path; mastership is the destination.

***

You can spend your time looking *out there* and blaming the world for your troubles or revert your gaze to discover your inner beauty. It is the call that each person makes that sets up the grandiosity of his experiences and life. Taking on the discipline to know who you are and access inner knowing takes you on a journey. It is akin to transforming a lumbering caterpillar to a stunning butterfly clothed in sparkling array and flying free. Indeed, this process is a metamorphosis. To identify with your True Self is nothing less than magic. It is your path whether you choose to take it now or later.

The following sections are relevant to the process. They will lift your mind to a level of compassion, which is music to the soul. Compassion and kindness are forms of love. You need love, kindness, compassion, and forgiveness to become your greatest Self. Through this metamorphose process you are conditioning the mind to experience the nurturing quality of the soul. In this practice you release the energy of aggressive masculine action and intellectualism and cultivate the softer qualities of love and kindness. To operate from the vastness of Spirit, the mind must be receptive, and open.

Kindness, compassion, gratitude, and forgiveness are heart-felt energies that produce strong inner connection. You cannot engage them without strengthening heart-energy and intuition. The desire to serve, to make a difference, is the natural outcome of this type of transformation. These are the elements that move you beyond the ego to your True Self, which means living in a state of connection. It is the way to knowing.

The world is your playground. To let go and relax denotes expanding your view of possibilities. There is a higher (finer) way to live life. By practicing the principles in this book, you have everything you need to keep your energy high/elevated. This automatically ignites passion and joy. In other words, you will feel great. Everything is possible, available, and fun.

Use these practices to keep your energy high and your mind in a state of knowing.

***

Gratitude Keeps Your Heart Open

When we blame our discomfort on others, we are heading in the opposite direction of inner knowing. Looking out there and blaming others keeps your energy low and stuck. You feel powerless. Gratitude, on the other hand, opens your heart, elevating dynamism.

Cultivating gratitude centers, you in the heart. It expands your energy and plants you into the present moment. It is a form of mental conditioning whereby you view life from a higher perspective, while transforming habitual thinking from limitation and what's wrong to positivity and what is possible. It prepares you to KNOW the truth.

Getting started involves releasing the force of aggressive masculine action and intellectualism. This helps you to move to your center and feel your deepest essence, which is love. Accepting love as your primary energy leads you smack dab into the vastness of Inner

Knowing. To achieve this state, the mind must be soft and receptive.

To illustrate how this is done, consider this wonderful legend. It is about a wanderer in the desert who happened on a spring of clear, fresh water. He is most excited to share his wonderful discovery and enthusiastically fills his jug with this water. His aim is to hurry off to share his precious treasure with his beloved king. The wanderer crosses a great distance, over many days, and eventually arrived at the palace to offer his gift to the king.

The king tasted the water and smiled. He then offered profuse thanks to the wanderer for his wonderful gift. The members of the court rushed forward to also sample the water. They were expecting to taste cool, clean water. Instead, they found the water to be hot and stale. They gagged and spit it out.

A member of the court inquired of the king, *"How could you give thanks for this spoiled water?"*

The king smiled broadly as he divulged that it was not the water he tasted, but the spirit in which it was given. The king was grateful for the loving intent of the wanderer.

Receiving a gift is an art unto itself. Remembering that it is not the gift but the spirit of the giver that counts can help us be better givers and receivers, and thereby cultivate the attitude of gratitude.

Gratitude may sound simple, yet it is not always practiced. When most people gaze about and perceive all they have achieved and accomplished, both tangible and intangible, instead of feeling awed and appreciative, they frequently think, *Is that all?* Or, *But I don't have that thing, event, or relationship I want.* Or, *What's next?* In other words, stopping to smell the roses is not part of the equation.

Do you consciously appreciate your friends, your family, your home, your job, your freedom, your health, the money you've earned? It is easy to take these things for granted and think that what you have isn't enough.

"My car isn't a BMW. It's an old Chevrolet."

"I'm not president of the company. I'm only _____ [fill in the blank]."

"I don't make enough money, have enough prestige, live in the best part of town, or know the right people."

With this kind of thinking, attention is not on what you have, but on what you do not have. It is on what is missing, on the negatives rather than the positives. It is called *fear-based* thinking. You never win or feel good about yourself when you focus on lack and live in fear.

Yet, the old car transports you wherever you want to go, and many people don't even own a car. Your current job is a stepping-stone to wherever you go from here. The house you own represents the down payment on the next one. All your past learning experiences graduate you to the next level and prepare you for greater expression and service. You will more easily move to your next car, job, home, and elevated opportunities by graciously appreciating the ones you already have and had.

The law of gratitude dictates that you value your current job position and customers. By doing this, new opportunities and customers readily present themselves.

Gratitude is a law of nature. When we accept and are at peace with our circumstances, things begin to change naturally, easily. Sincere gratitude sows the seeds that blossom in abundance. It is a principle of nature and it is magnetic.

When people feel acknowledged and appreciated, they more readily acknowledge and appreciate you. When you are grateful for all you have experienced and achieved, even the *bad* stuff, your life expands. Your understanding that hardship and challenge build the characteristics of strength and leadership becomes apparent. You need these qualities to achieve whatever goal you desire.

There is a science to gratitude. As you explore the energy of gratitude, you will discover a great law of prosperity. When you genuinely feel grateful, your energy rises and expands. It aligns with your Divinity. It connects you to God.

You can even feel it. Think of something or someone for which you are grateful. Notice the feeling in your body as you do this. It feels light and expanded.

Now consider someone or something for which you feel annoyed, angry, resentful, or critical. You will notice your body shifting to a restricted state. The energy is tight. It might even burn because anger is inflamed energy.

Be sure to bring yourself back to gratitude. As you observe more and more, your choice will be gratitude. You have the ability and responsibility to choose where you place your mind. You must develop the discipline to keep it focused on where you want it to be. That means what outcome do you desire. The mind has no choice but to abide by your wishes.

For the most part, people do not recognize that they have this ability. This kind of mental training alters the projector of your life. As your projector changes, your life follows suit. Be willing to train your thoughts, and you will find the benefits astounding.

When you generate thoughts of gratefulness, it is equivalent to having already received. Gratitude for having already received your desire immediately magnetizes the energy needed to manifest it in your space-time reality.

The Quantum Field of energy, that in which we live, breath, and have our being, receives the impressions of your thoughts. As stated earlier, it is mutable, like Silly Putty. It automatically assumes the shape, intensity, and quality of your thoughts. In other words, your thoughts are a template for this mutable energy to take form.

Magnetic thoughts of gratitude expand energy and bring more of what you appreciate to you.

To say it another way, gratitude shifts Universal energy. It manipulates it so that the ideas, hunches, connections, and opportunities you need are drawn to you. That is how your desires are made manifest.

Reverend Michael Beckwith says it this way, *"You cannot have what you are not willing to be vibrationally."* You must match the vibration of that which you desire.

Oprah Winfrey, the great television personality, demonstrates a good example of the workings of this law. She began life living with her grandmother, a maid in Mississippi in a house without indoor plumbing. Her grandmother wanted to train her to be a maid so she could work for a good "white" family. Oprah wasn't having it. She had her own dreams…bigger dreams.

Winfrey always excelled in school and had a natural ability to speak to others. For instance, she would recite the Sunday sermon to her classmates on Monday. She used her intelligence and innate skills for communication to move beyond her meager beginnings. She sought education and opportunity, and ended up creating a life of influence, wealth, and success.

Throughout her development, Oprah kept a *Gratitude Journal*. At the end of each day, she recorded all the things for which she was grateful. She daily acknowledged the people she met, what she learned, and each event that encouraged her growth. And now, she has made history as the first black female to become a billionaire. She is an icon!

Universal law states that what you focus on increases. Oprah focused on gratitude and, through the law of increase, her position, opportunities, friendships, and wealth increased. She started working at a news desk and ended up owning her own cable television network. Her life is abundant. Yours can be, too.

This law of increase is indiscriminate and works for everyone. Start your day with appreciation for all the opportunities at hand and end your day with gratitude for all you have experienced and all you have given and received. Also be grateful for the seeming dark times. We need those to wake up. *Thank you for this incredible opportunity to grow and be more than I was before. Thank you for unleashing me.*

One woman I know takes a trip to the grocery store whenever she begins to doubt the law of abundance. As she stands and gazes over the myriad types of fruits and vegetables, she is reminded how truly great the world is. She sees abundance in the dozens of different breads, every kind of meat, aisles filled with condiments, a bakery full of desserts. Staggering abundance. Perhaps visiting a grocery store can remind you of abundance as well.

What a great world we live in. We have endless opportunities to express, experience, live freely, laugh, love, share, and experience every kind of abundance. If something doesn't work, make a different choice, and get to your goal another way. There are many routes to the same destination.

As you make gratitude your everyday experience, you will attract greater and greater potentials into your life. You will develop the determination to climb over obstacles and blast through walls. You will become unstoppable and your energy will expand and soar. All along the way your intuitive voice will guide you. As you take each step along the adventure called your life, your inner knowing becomes strong.

The dynamic power of gratitude opens you to the field of possibilities. Elizabeth Gilbert, author of *Eat, Pray, Love,* suggests, *"You need to learn how to select your thoughts just the same way you select your clothes every day. This is a power you can cultivate. If you want to control things in your life so bad, work on the mind. That's the only thing you should be trying to control."*

Activity

1. Start a gratitude journal and record your blessings every morning and evening, or at least every night before you go to bed. At night, while you sleep, your mind will build on your gratitude list to create the events for the next day.

2. Begin each day with statements of gratitude.
   I am grateful for this magnificent day and my continuous blessings.
   I am grateful for sunshine and a great meeting with my boss.
   I am grateful for nutritious food and fun friends.
   Thank you for the beautiful trees, grass, and flowers.
   Keep going. Make the list new every day.

3.   Notice the changes that occur in your life. Observe the blessings that show up. Perhaps someone buys your meal or brings you coffee. You may receive a great coupon for your favorite store. Someone invites you to a party. The birds are singing joyfully. The sunset is gorgeous.

***

Service is Love in Action

It is said that the happiest people are the ones who serve others. There is a reason for that. Service is the way we set the ego aside and rise to soul fulfillment. To take a break from your own needs and recognize that the world needs you is humbling and rewarding at the same time. Service expands your energy, validates your gifts, and moves you to highest expression. Service accomplished with right intention connects you to your higher mind of deep, inner knowing.

Albert Schweitzer said it well. *I don't know what your destiny will be, but one thing I know. The only ones among you who will be truly happy are those who have sought and found how to serve.*

This chapter touches on two principles, service and surrender, which are necessary to live a life of mastership, which means knowing. You may have seen the bumper sticker, *God is the driver and I am the passenger,* or some variation of the same idea. This speaks of releasing control of your life to something greater than your small self. It means that you are to move into second position and become the helpmate to Universal Intelligence.

The idea of relinquishing the driver's seat does not diminish your importance, because each person provides a necessary vehicle or channel by which it all comes together. In other words, the universe uses each one of us to channel energy for the greater good of all.

These two principles of service and surrender work together. To truly be of service in the world, you must surrender your opinions, beliefs, and biases, and be open to spiritual input being directed in, to, and as you in the form of ideas, inspiration, words, and actions

As we moved through all the principles provided in this book, we have prepared for the opportunity to be used in a greater way.

By developing non-resistance and non-attachment, learning to love without condition, releasing judgments, embracing aloneness, understanding gratitude, magnetism, and entrainment, we have prepared to become suitable instruments, receptive to channel the highest spiritual energy.

As you learn to concentrate, and then meditate, your mind becomes sharper, clearer, and more open to Spirit. Answers come more easily. Struggles dissipate. You develop laser focus and clarity, which allows the Universal forces to consolidate with purpose.

Once you have trained your mind, you find that whatever you focus on shows up in your life. You can accomplish any objective. You are unstoppable. You recognize that your lessons have been stepping-stones to guide you along to greater strength, knowing, and vision.

Service is the ultimate destination. It acknowledges the oneness of all life. Being in service brings bountiful joy and greatest connection to Spirit.

Additionally, giving to others builds self-esteem. As you give your talents and energy away with the focus on helping, you are expressing your highest consciousness. This extends your energy beyond the small egoic self. As others feel better, so do you. You naturally feel good when you realize that you have had a positive impact in the world. This is the power in service.

Service is the way you recognize the value of your gifts; that this earth trip is not just about intellectualism and accumulation but about expansion through living a great purpose. Whether your service is about binding wounds, inspiring higher thought, keeping great accounting records, mopping the floor, cradling a baby, or cooking a hamburger, all are important, and all add to the sum total of wholeness and balance in this earth plane. As you serve, you become a mini sun, radiating your light to the world. The light that you share may be as simple as holding a door for someone, or carrying their groceries, or as magnificent as bringing medical help, food, or education to third-world nations. Your service will resonate with you and your specific talents. All are important.

To serve means to focus on the big picture. How can I bring more love into the world?

Oprah Winfrey prays daily that God will use her for His purpose.

As you address this question of service, your small ego-self and its problems, worries and, challenges cease to pull at you because your attention is elsewhere. Reaching out to assist others brings out the best in you, and that becomes a truth for you. You begin to realize who you really are an exalted spiritual being. As your attention, focus, and effort are dedicated to a goal greater than small ego-gratification, your consciousness elevates. It is a mini vacation from your micro self and the path to knowing. Anytime you elevate your attention beyond your small world, you enter the realm of Spiritual energy, and that is knowing.

Here is a story that illustrates this point. During a tense period in St. Louis, when there was a conflict between the police and the citizens, four families determined to bring healing to their community. They set out to help the police create a positive impression. They joined together and collected $36,200, which they gave to the police to pass out to the citizens as they saw fit.

On a Tuesday in December 2016, city and county police officers surprised the citizens by handing out thousands of $100 bills. The shocked recipients were amazed and appreciative of the tables being turned in this positive way. Instead of traffic tickets an summons, they were handed money.

The compassion shown by the participating police officers in the giveaway was reciprocated with hugs and thanks all around. The event created a huge upward shift in police citizen relationships and even made national news.

Joseph Higgs of St. Louis, when trying to leave his house in his van to take his children to the library, was blocked by a patrol car. He got out of his car to talk to the officers. They told him, *"Merry Christmas,"* and handed him the money.

Higgs said it was like, *"Take this money and keep being a good citizen."* He felt the experience improved relations with law enforcement. *"What helps my opinion is how jovial they were in doing it. They were still professional and jovial, and they were doing their job and doing it in a good way."*

The four families, who chose to remain anonymous, donated the money for the Secret Santa Project because they were heartbroken over recent events in their community and wanted to bring people together. Subsequently, they created a windfall for some ordinary citizens and great joy for the officers who took part.

These simple acts of caring turn the tide of anger and resentment to love.

Emily is another example of a person transformed through service. She came to me because she was depressed and anxious. She had lost the job she had held for many years. As her company downsized, Emily felt like a ship without a rudder or a port. For her, it was not a great job: answering phones, performing some computer work, and keeping records. It wasn't inspirational or particularly fulfilling, but she did get a paycheck.

As I got to know Emily, she admitted that she never had a passion for anything, nor had a career vision or something she was driven to do, but she always liked helping people.

We decided to build on her love of helping others. First, to deal with depression, Emily had to come to terms with the idea that losing her unfulfilling job was not a great deficit. Her greater loss, in her estimation, was not having structure in her life. She felt adrift without a plan or a place to go. The disposition of the paycheck was really more about the cultural idea that to be paid money equated to having value. On closer investigation, there were other ways to be paid that did not involve money. That is what Emily was about to discover.

Emily started listening to her heart and, when it spoke, she took action. She had always enjoyed working at the community food pantry, handing out groceries to people in need, people who were highly appreciative. She decided to increase her hours at the pantry. She found another charity that assisted young girls in obtaining party dresses so they could attend school dances and proms. She helped this group get organized and devised efficient methods to serve more young ladies.

Plus, Emily loved books and she found a bookstore that needed help. It seemed that Emily had a niche discovering community needs and filling them, because next, she volunteered at a home for older folks and visited weekly with some of the residents. They loved that and so did she.

In a few months, Emily's anxiety about *not working* and her depression over not feeling valued was gone. In its place was a radiant woman with a beautiful smile and a heart filled with joy. The weight she had lost earlier due to worry was being slowly replaced, and that was a good thing.

Emily has strong faith and she knew she had been guided to her new life. The structure she needed was of her own making. Tuesdays and Thursdays, she put smiles on people's faces as she handed out broccoli and turkey at the pantry. Mondays, she helped at the prom-dress charity.

Fridays, she visited the older adults, and so on. In the middle of all this, she took care of herself with yoga and spending quiet time at a local chapel.

The last time we visited, Emily beamed brightly. *"I have the best job in the world and my payment is personal fulfillment."*

That is how fulfillment works. Instead of fighting the circumstances, Emily explored possibilities for self-expression. She discovered the blessings in losing her job, because that is how she found her true work. For Emily, service was the path to contentment and joy.

Leo Tolstoy said, *Life is a place of service. Joy can be real only if people look upon their life as a service and have a definite object in life outside themselves and their personal happiness.*

If you are not enjoying your life, you can either change your attitude or change your work. Often, a job change is the less desirable alternative. So instead, look for ways to serve others while you are doing your work. Or do work that serves others.

There is really no job or career that doesn't include service. You can incorporate service into your life, no matter what your occupation. The level of success that each person demonstrates is in direct proportion to that person's desire to truly serve others. If you are dishing up hamburgers and fries, you can do it with the attitude of helping people. If you are an actor performing on stage, you can embrace your work with the intention of providing entertainment, joy, and diversion for your audience. Great salespeople provide service in fulfilling needs. In all cases, you can do what you do with love.

Beyond the reward of increasing sales, the person who seeks to help people achieves a happier, easier life is exercising the highest type of salesmanship. Meeting needs with highest integrity leaves an impression like a rock thrown into a pond. Anything done with love has a ripple effect. Thereby, you recognize that the opportunity to serve, i.e., shine your light, is present at all times, whether you make sales, serve up fast food, or simply smile at people. With each act you send out a ripple of love.

Service is a natural partner to surrender. One of the ways we complicate our lives is by thinking of ourselves as separate from each other and the universe. This belief is so prevalent that it is necessary to continually remind ourselves that we are an integral part of a universal puzzle, and that our individual power is derived from this connectedness.

That is to say, the power we experience as individuals is the power of the universe. It continually flows through us to be expressed. Consequently, the more we open to this inherent flow and perfection, the more fun and freedom we experience. We open to the flow of love and recognize it in all people. We are one family. Assuming an attitude of service enriches and fulfills our lives. That is what Emily discovered, and it is what you will discover, too.

The opportunity to live our lives and express love and joy is our greatest privilege, and like any privilege, it must be cherished in order to make the best use of it. Every time you open your heart to assist another, you experience this favor and learn again that life is a magnificent gift.

One of the reasons we can easily embrace surrender is that we know that the universe handles the details. This was exemplified for the police who needed an infusion of community support and the families ready to help them get it. Emily needed her right work to feel fulfilled.

The universe supplied the solutions.

Much of the time, we believe that handling the details is a conscious-mind activity and we must figure it out. This is generally an attempt to figure out the best way to get from here to there, approach a situation, or plan the achievement of an objective. However, the conscious mind does not know all the variables in any situation. Only Infinite Intelligence has this information. So, even though we think we know enough to plan everything, we often find our plans delusional and, they may even get in the way of a successful conclusion.

As we turn over this *how* function to Infinite Intelligence, things seem to fall in place perfectly. If we follow our intuitive guide, our Source provides the urges, messages, and guidance, without effort on our part. Then it is matter of taking right action.

For example, everyone has had the experience of going to a place because it felt right to go there. Then, what seemed like a chance meeting produced a valuable connection. As we reflect on this, we realize that there was no way we could have planned that meeting or met that person, whose existence wasn't even known to us. The universe managed the details perfectly.

Now, let's consider how to apply these principles of service and surrender.

Activity

1. Each day start with a conversation with God or the universe. Ask for help and include thankfulness. *Help me to be of greatest service today. Thank you for ongoing assistance in every area of my life. Thank you for showing me the ways I can serve your purpose today. Thank you for using me for the highest good. Thank you for helping me with my project. I know that you are working out the details for everything to be brought to its highest conclusion. Thank you for giving me abundance and prosperity in all my endeavors. Thank you for your guidance in helping me give my light and love to others and to receive theirs. I am grateful for all the ways you love me. I feel blessed!*

2. Go about your business. Do the things you have to do and, in the doing of them, pay attention. If you are wondering about your purpose in life, do whatever is in front of you to be done. By paying attention, you will run right into your purpose.

3. Pay attention. The messages and guidance come intuitively and that is subtle energy. Guidance shows up in the people you meet, the books you are drawn to read, the symbols that appear before you. Listen to your heart. What are you feeling? Pay attention. It is relevant. When something feels right, do it. It may or may not be your ultimate course but will definitely lead to your right path.

4. Take action. Take the action that comes to you from your guidance. Do it and let go. See where it takes you and start again with number 1 above. When you follow the directions given from your guidance, do not concern yourself with where it takes you.

5. Give thanks! Give thanks! Give thanks!

***

Cultivate Connection as a Daily Practice

Often people read inspirational books and listen to empowering lectures and still don't know how to put the principles into action in their lives. The idea of adjusting their thoughts and beliefs seem overwhelming. In this section, I give you step-by-step instructions on developing a daily practice that will deepen your spiritual knowing and make connecting to Spirit simple, easy, and doable. The ego wants to make everything hard; Spirit knows all the short cuts. Morning Practice – ten minutes

1. Start with gratitude – name at least three things you are grateful for today. Make these different each day. This sets your energy HIGH! Example:

    I am grateful that I am free to make my own decisions and express myself creatively.
    I am grateful for loving friends and family and laughter.
    I am grateful that my home is well organized.

2. Affirm to God: Please use me in your highest way today. Help me to channel your love to everyone I meet. (By affirming, always in the positive, you are setting a clear intention. The mind always follows positive intention.)

3. Meditate: Sit quietly and observe your breath coming in and going out. Observe the space between the in and out breath and notice the stillness. Do this for five minutes. As you acclimate to the stillness, you can expand your meditation time and even take on a theme, such as: How can I love more deeply? Or, help me to understand the nature of love.

By giving yourself quiet, focused time, your mind will clear, and your neurological system will heal. Our daily rushing and stressing is hard on the nervous system. Meditation, on the other hand, sooths and heals.

Midday practice: ten minutes

Set aside ten minutes in the midday to breath. Do at least five deep breaths and concentrate on clearing your mental slate. Stating affirmations facilitates this process. Example:

> *I am invigorated and filled with gratitude and love.*
> *I am strong and capable. I move easily through each task.*
> *I am happy!*

(If there is no place to do this mini break at work, sit in your car and quiet your mind. If there is a challenge you are dealing with, affirm that you have the resources and assistance you need to manage it easily and conclude successfully.)

Evening Practice – ten minutes

1. Start with gratitude. Name at least three things for which you are grateful from this day.

    Example:

    Thank you for a productive meeting with my boss (client, co-worker, etcetera.)

    Thank you for this beautiful sunshiny day, fresh air, and gorgeous sunset.

    Thank you for the inspiration of exquisite flowers and trees as I drive to and from work.

    Thank you for my strong body and vibrant health.

2. For better sleep, write all the things you want to remember for tomorrow. This is kind of a *To-Do* list. The idea is to purge your mind, so you won't be bothered with these items while you are healing and recharging during sleep.

Also, rewind your mind by remembering everything you did during the day, from the last activity to the first. You can write this down or just remember each thing. Do this no longer than five minutes. This will clear your mind so you will be able to achieve deep, restorative sleep.

3. Meditate for five minutes. You can imagine a beautiful, brilliant light coming toward you and engulfing your heart area and spreading throughout your body and beyond. Feel that you are in a gigantic bubble of light. Then imagine it filling the entire room and then the house. Feel this light as love and relax into it. Breathe into the light and imagine your body slowly disappearing and you are the light and the light is everything.

When you are finished go to bed. (NEVER meditate in bed. Meditation is a technique to increase your awareness. If you meditate in bed, it becomes a technique to relax and sleep and you will lose the potential to increase your awareness and deepen intuition.)

Additionally, as you progress and your energy lightens and your mind becomes clearer, you will want to integrate forgiveness, acts of kindness, and service as daily practices. These activities do not have to be time-consuming or difficult. Forgiveness can be in the moment.

Someone cuts you off in traffic and you forgive him, his rush, and lack of consideration. You hold no baggage or toxic energy as you do this.

Kindness can be as easy as smiling at people and service is as simple as helping someone with their packages, offering positive affirmation or a pat on the back.

Soon, these practices become habitual and your energy soars – you have not only lifted your consciousness but affected everyone around you as well. The world begins to glisten.

Conclusion

Love is everything. It is the key to life, and its influences are those that move the world.

Ralph Waldo Emerson

If you want to predict the future, create it (in your mind) first!

Peter Drucker

Summary:

As you gain experience and practice and understand the principles and exercises described in this book, you will develop the spiritual gifts of higher vision, intuition, shifting fear to love, managing emotions, and deep listening to know the truth. Expressing from your heart elevates your energy and creates magnetism. This simply means that anything and everything is possible. These are the heavenly treasures that do not rust or decay and bless you every day

*** .

There are many amazing people who accomplish great things, but do not know how to be happy. Intellectualism will not bring you to a high vibrational energy level. Practicing spiritual principles will. With these you can train your mind to operate in high-energy frequency.

Intuitive knowing, clarity and confidence results.

You have explored different concepts and exercises to elevate your consciousness to become a being of magnetism and love. To live in the world, yet not be of the world means practicing this art of intuitive connection in every circumstance. To ask, what is the real meaning of this? Or, what is my highest purpose (in any situation) helps you gain perspective. With continuous practice, you develop a strong center and clarity.

We live in an aggressive, even pushy, world. Getting things done, physical activity, accomplishment, completing the *to-do* list – these have been dominant themes drilled into our psyches. They are fine unto themselves. But they are not enough. Without inner awareness and connection, none of it matters much. In other words, you make millions, travel internationally, own multiple houses, and take magnificent vacations, but, in the end, if you are bereft of the peace that comes with Spiritual connection, what have you really accomplished? What do you take with you when you leave the earth?

By cultivating intuition and inner knowing, you become spiritually invincible. Achieving this objective is worth investing time, energy, and practice. These treasures do not rust or rot.

They glean you the greatest rewards of your life –peace, stability, and confidence.

Being able to lift your energy and perceive a higher dimension at will releases worry and anxiety. The ability to understand yourself and other people through compassionately acknowledging their wounds, frees you. Learning to love without cause, forgiving with ease, and being grateful insures happiness. These are the skills that keep you consciously united to the great field of energy called the universe. Awareness is the by-product.

The ability to listen deeply must be cultivated. It requires mind training and willingness. Every technique and method outlined in this book is for the express purpose of helping you develop this crucial skill.

Listen deeply to the stillness between breaths or between thoughts. Move into this stillness and sense the inner spaciousness. Guidance will emerge. It is all about love. Love is the only constant – the only reality.

Living from love makes you magnetic. Miracles become regular occurrences. The only reason you have not consented to miracles before is because you have accepted the indoctrinated, learned beliefs of limitation taught you as a child. They have kept you small and judgmental. Moving beyond restrictive ideas into the expansiveness of Spirit makes everything possible – including miracles. Expect them; ask for them; they are yours!

All art, music, design, inventions and every creative idea exist within consciousness. It is already there. Our work as we become more Spiritually minded is to open to this creativity. We might think that by making this change we will increase our wealth, health, and personal relationships and that will happen. But what is more important is that you will manifest enlightenment and every aspect of life is enhanced. We live in a higher frequency of energy.

We live more freely, love abundantly, and joy becomes our natural state.

The truth is that you cannot increase your consciousness because you already have everything. What you can do is open more fully to the infinity within you. That is how you gain a Spiritual sense of existence.

Opening your channel is a choice, a decision. You open this channel in much the same way as you choose which radio station you want to listen to. You set a frequency and you are essentially "tuned in." By keeping your channel open to Spirit (intuition), you increase awareness. You wake up in much the same way as Buddha stating, *"I am awake."*

When he spoke those words, he was not referring to waking from sleep, but from the hypnotic trance of limited physical existence. He woke up to the truth of who he was – a spiritual being inhabiting a physical body yet possessing the power of choice.

That is what we endeavor to do in this book. Wake up to the incredible power and brilliance that lies within. It is present in everyone. As you make the choice to do the work, immediately the quality of life improves. Intentionality to allow the flow of light and love into your consciousness alters everything. As you identify with Spirit, change happens miraculously. Without resistance or attachment, you flow with life and know where to go, who to speak to, and what to say. You exhibit joy. Not because you have increased your net worth (although, you might have), but because bringing more light into the world is joyful. And as the saying goes, when you keep your eye (your I AM, your focus) single, all else is given unto you. Life becomes joyful and extravagance. Friendship deepens, trust widens, health and disposition improve. In other words, all else is given unto you.

As I close this book, I offer you a blessing: May each day bring you deepened awareness and greater light that translates to clarity, confidence and peace. Shall each experience and relationship bless you with heightened understanding and transcendence.

###

Thank you for reading The Power of Knowing: *8 Step Guide to Open Your Intuitive Channel and Live in Highest Consciousness - Clarity, peace, power and transformation*

Can you help get the word out about this book by writing a review? Amazon.com loves reviews and endorses books that have them. Please go to Amazon.com and put the name of this book and author in the search box and click on review or stars to write your review. Was there a main point or message you received from this book? Please let me know. I am eternally grateful for your help!!! Jean Walters

Would you opt in to hear about the next book? You can go to my website: http://www.spiritualtransformation.com and sign up for my newsletter (front page) and I will keep you in touch with the latest happenings and specials. Thank you, again for staying in touch.

Jean Walters, DM, DD, CRT
http://www.spiritualformation.com
jean@spiritualtransformation.com

About the author:

Jean Walters has been at the forefront in the movement for personal transformation, clarity and truth for over 40 years. Through her writings, consulting, coaching, and Akashic Record Readings for people all over the world, she has been a consistent source of light, clarity, and inspiration. Jean's intention and commitment to deepest truth have brought her to share her wisdom and guidance to tens of thousands of clients and students.

As a leading authority on metaphysics, she promotes deep spiritual connection and enlightenment. She has authored articles and columns in major newspapers and magazines all over the United States and is a best-selling author on Amazon.com. Her books include:

- Set Yourself Free: Live the Life YOU were Meant to Live!
- Be Outrageous: Do the Impossible – Others Have and You can too! (Find Your Passion)
- The Journey from Anxiety to Peace: Practical Steps to Handle Fear, Embrace Struggle and Eliminate Worry to become Happy and Free
- Dreams and the Symbology of Life

Walters has designed and presented classes and workshops on empowerment, meditation, building communication skills, universal laws, dreams interpretation, strengthening intuition, and creating spiritual connection for many organizations, colleges, universities, spiritual groups, and businesses. She continues to offer her services to empower others.

She is the recipient of The Marquis Who's Who Lifetime Achievement Award and listed in Who's Who 35 times. You can find her books on Amazon.com

From her office in Saint Louis, Missouri, she works with people around the world as a Transformational Coach and Akashic Record reader. She has performed over 35,000 readings with the emphasis on providing insight regarding personal growth, life purpose, strengthening relationships, and moving through obstacles. She has been presented with "Best Psychic in Saint Louis Award for the six years.

Walters' mission is to lead people to the Light – to encourage,

guide and assist others to live freely and express from their Highest
Selves. You can reach her through her website.

Jean Walters, DM, DD, CRT
http://www.spiritualtransformation.com

Other titles from Higher Ground Books & Media:

Wise Up to Rise Up by Rebecca Benston

A Path to Shalom by Steen Burke

Overcomer by Forrest Henslee

Miracles: I Love Them by Forest Godin

Out of Darkness by Stephen Bowman

Dear You by Derra Nicole Sabo

I Don't Want to Be Like You by Maryanne Christiano-Mistretta

Shameless Persistence by Sandra Bretting

Jack Kramer's Journey by Frank Adkins

Chronicles of a Spiritual Journey by Stephen Shepherd

The Real Prison Diaries by Judy Frisby

The Silent Destruction by Yasmin S. Brown

Add these titles to your collection today!

http://www.highergroundbooksandmedia.com

Do you have a story to tell?

Higher Ground Books & Media is an independent Christian-based publisher specializing in stories of triumph! Our purpose is to empower, inspire, and educate through the sharing of personal experiences.

Please visit our website for our submission guidelines.

http://www.highergroundbooksandmedia.com

Made in the USA
Monee, IL
09 March 2020